30119 014131389
LONDON BOROUGH OF SUTTON

D1766887

The Banbury and Cheltenham Railway 1887–1962

Chipping Norton

The Banbury and Cheltenham Railway 1887–1962

J. H. Russell

Oxford Publishing Co.

SBN 902888 45 5

Looking towards Chipping Norton Tunnel.

Printed by Blackwell's
in the City of Oxford

Photo-Reproduction and Offset Plates by
Oxford Litho Plates Limited, Oxford.

Typesetting by Gem Graphic Services
Didcot, Oxon.

Published by
Oxford Publishing Co.
8 The Roundway
Headington, Oxford

Introduction

Many small books have already been published, dealing with some of the small attractive branch lines of the old Great Western Railway. One notable exception, however, has been the long, meandering, single line which ran from Banbury on the London-Birmingham main line, crossed the Oxford-Worcester line at Kingham, and finally joined the Birmingham-South Wales line at Cheltenham.

It has given me great pleasure to undertake this task, as, not only am I in the privileged position of having actually worked over the branch for many years, but also I have photographed the line extensively, and created a 4mm. scale model railway based on this 'Chipping Norton' railway.

My approach is probably slightly different to that of other authors. The history is condensed into a primary section, whilst the secondary part is taken up with an imaginary journey over the branch, beginning at Banbury and continuing through to Kingham, and finally on to Cheltenham, mentioning anything of interest which used to be on this Cotswold line, just as I remember it. I can still recall many unique features of the branch, so that a reasonable record of the 47 miles can be placed on paper before time and memory erases all that has gone before, and which seemed so permanent at the time!

Contents

Map of the Line . . . 2
History . . . 3
Along the route . . . 11
- Banbury . . . 11
- Kings Sutton . . . 17
- Adderbury . . . 23
- Milton Halt . . . 26
- Bloxham . . . 28
- Hook Norton . . . 36
- Rollright Halt . . . 46
- Chipping Norton . . . 48
- Sarsden Halt . . . 62
- Kingham . . . 65
- Stow on the Wold . . . 81
- Bourton on the Water . . . 84
- Notgrove . . . 93
- Andoversford . . . 98
- Charlton Kings . . . 106
- Cheltenham South & Leckhampton . . . 110
- Cheltenham Malvern Road . . . 114
- Cheltenham St. James . . . 116

Timetables . . . 121
Motive Power . . . 124
Locomotive Diagrams . . . 135

Adderbury station depicting 0-6-0 Pannier Tank No. 5404 departing with an Auto-car.

Map of the line

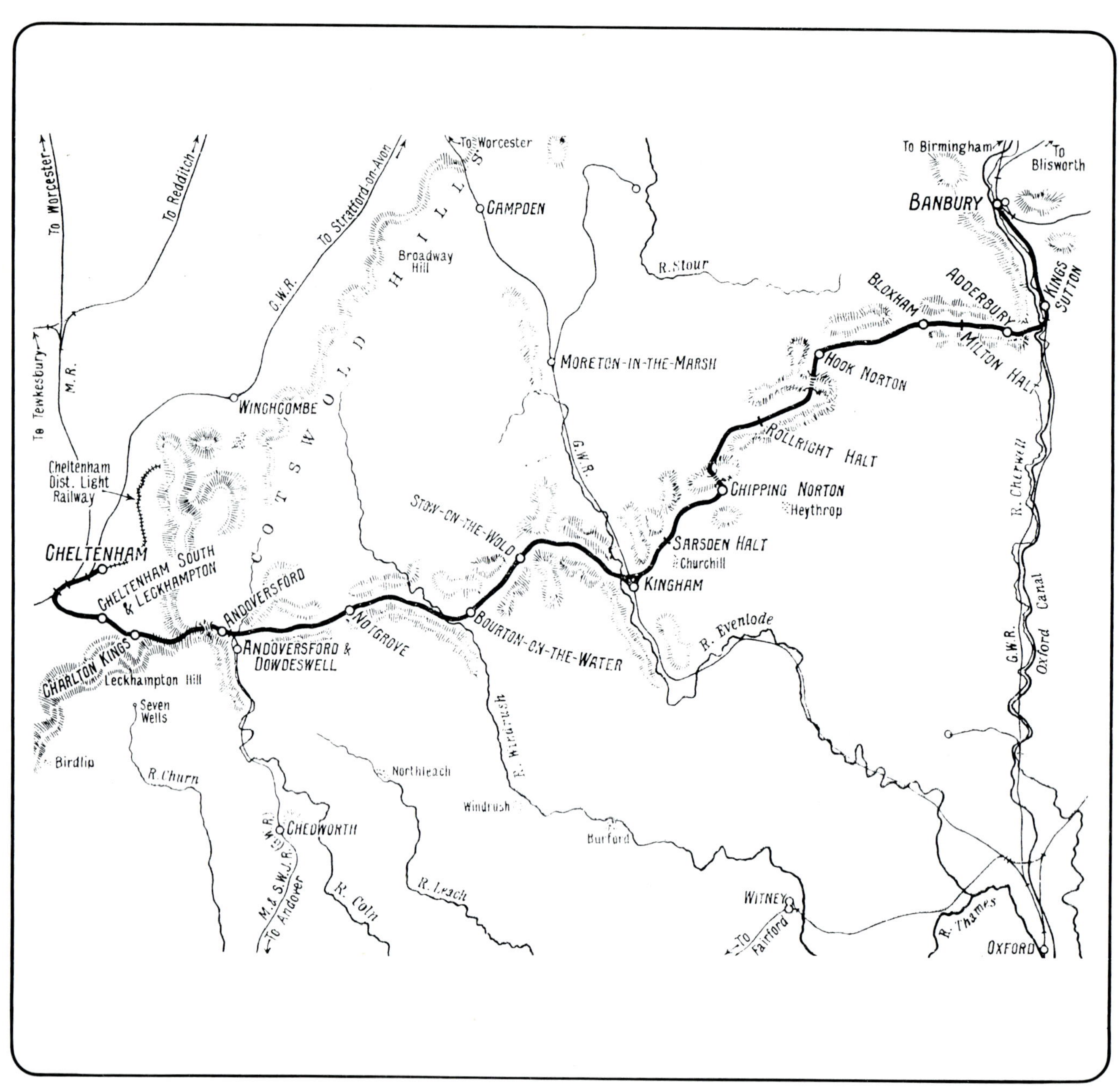

Acknowledgements

I gratefully acknowledge the help of the following in allowing me to include the photographs listed below.

British Railways *Figs 1-6, 115, 142, 143, 145, 147, 152-157, 162, 185, 200, 229, 242, 246:* Roger Carpenter *Figs 12, 13, 23, 170, 171:* M. W. Earley *Fig 233:* Michael Hale *Figs 11, 15, 18, 52, 80, 94, 110, 112, 117, 119, 148, 159, 187, 201, 211, 213-16, 219, 222, 227:* H. G. W. Household *Figs 202-209:* Lens of Sutton *Figs 14, 16, 158, 218, 224:* L & GRP *Figs 7-10, 57, 113, 120, 172, 186, 210, 217, 225, 226, 230, 235, 236, 238-240:* C. G. Maggs *Figs 17, 197-199, 212, 223:* Packers Studio *Figs 239-43, 48, 91-93, 98-101:* Rev. G. D. Parkes *Pages 11 & 124:* R. H. G. Simpson *Page 1.*

I should also like to thank George Pryer for supplying the signal box diagrams and Paul Karau for preparing our own track plans.

History

One of the longest 'Branch' lines of the old Great Western Railway was the 47 mile long Banbury-Cheltenham direct route, opened in 1887 and closed in 1962. The line was the culmination of 40 years planning by various interested bodies, with the object of linking Cheltenham cross-country to the main GWR Banbury-Oxford-London line, or even The Wash with the Bristol Channel.

The whole east-west route of this Cotswold railway was divided into four separate stages and dates, but the system from which it eventually grew was undoubtedly the old Oxford-Worcester and Wolverhampton Railway. So, to set the scene, perhaps a few explanatory words about the 'Old Worse and Worse' (as it was colloquially known) would help.

It was in 1853 that the OW&W had been opened in stages towards Oxford southwards, and originally was laid with a mixed gauge track of both 7′ and 4′ 8½″. The Great Western Railway, which had reached Oxford with the broad gauge in 1844, had ideas of extending its service north-westwards over this new line but had not reckoned with the fierce competition of its rival, the London and North Western Railway Co., who were also keen to seize on to any territory which might have proved of use to the opposition! *(See Map 1 of 1853.)*

Many schemes were mooted for linking up the LNWR, both at Oxford and Banbury, with the new OW&W Railway. In 1851 although pressurised by the GWR to lay in broad gauge, the new company agreed that it would also put in standard gauge to meet the LNWR entreaties. The OW&W also agreed that it would connect with a branch running from the LNWR at Banbury to join the new line at Moreton in Marsh. However, this scheme eventually failed and the OW&W Railway tried another tack and laid plans in Parliament in 1853 to bring in the 'Cheltenham and Oxford Union Railway'. This aimed to construct a railway from Yarnton in the south-east, near Oxford, through Witney, Barford and Northleach, over the Cotswold escarpment, into Cheltenham.

In the event, the Commons would have none of it, and the promotion suffered the same fate as another project of 1844, which was to run from Cheltenham, across the hills, easterly, and join the OW&W Railway at Shipton-under-Wychwood.

So, there was the scene: the principal mixed gauge railway in the centre, running from Oxford to Evesham and Worcester; on the eastward side, the broad gauge Paddington-Banbury GWR line plus the LNWR at both Oxford and Banbury; and in the west, the Midland and

Map 1

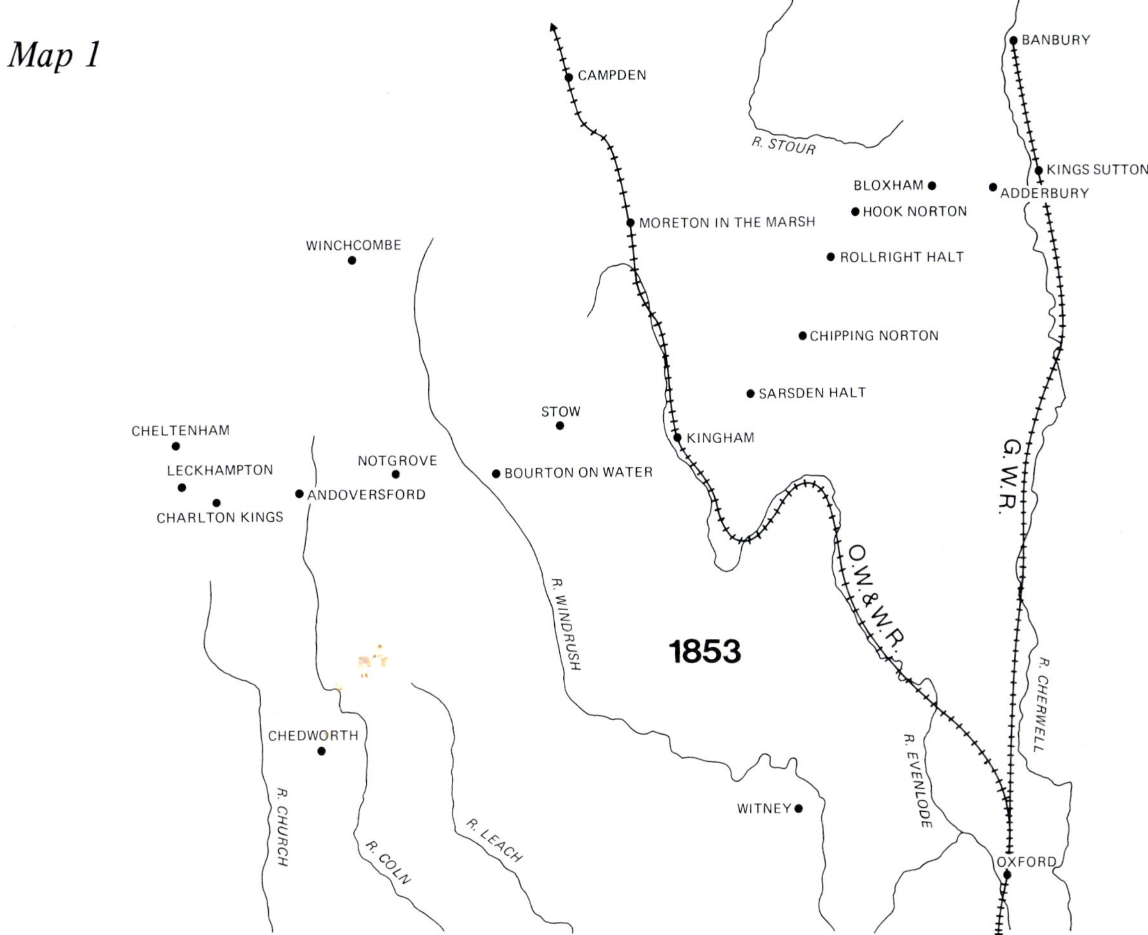

GWR both at Cheltenham. It was small wonder that local residents in the Spa area wanted to see a line linking their town with Oxford and, in consequence, London.

The LNWR were the first to "cash in" on the Oxford-Wolverhampton line by getting the OW&WR to build a branch at Oxford from their Buckingham Railway to a junction at Wolvercote. A through service from Euston-Worcester and Wolverhampton was inaugurated, which rather upset the GWR! To comply with the letter of their agreement with the GWR, one or two broad gauge trains did venture up the OW&W, one even as far as Tipton, but it was only a gesture and in 1858 all broad gauge rails were taken up south of Priestfield.

This is the brief outline of the beginnings of the OW&W Railway from which the Banbury-Cheltenham branch eventually developed. The first section was the short two-bridge branch of 4½ miles which ran from the OW&W Railway metals, to the Oxfordshire town of Chipping Norton.

Upon conducting any research into the Chipping Norton area, one is almost sure to be struck at once by the influence of William Bliss upon the town and its environs. This worthy gentleman was the owner of Bliss's Tweed Mills and astute enough to realize that the coming of the railway to the district meant two vital things to his business: first, transport of the finished cloth to buyers, and second, a supply of coal with which to change the water power at the mills to steam. At that time, 1840, the Cotswold area was still predominantly sheep country and although the wool trade was rapidly being shifted to Lancashire, Burford, Northleach, Witney and Chipping Norton were still wool towns. Hence, William Bliss had the raw material for his tweed shawls and military uniforms, grazing in the wolds all round the mills.

To entertain the idea of steam engines for working the looms, a supply of coal was vital and before the railway age this meant a long costly drag over the turnpike roads by wagon and horses, from the canal basic at Banbury, thirteen miles away. Small wonder, then, that this go-ahead mill owner, four times Mayor of a market town of 3,000 souls (second largest in the county to Oxford at that time), a Baptist, with the welfare of citizens and workers very much at heart, should have pressed for a rail link connecting Chipping Norton to the rapidly growing network of steam locomotion.

His first approaches were to the Oxford, Worcester and Wolverhampton Co. in 1846, but receiving no satisfaction with these feelers, he wrote again on September 23rd, 1847, direct to William Lewis, one of the OW&W's directors, as follows:

"Dear Sir,

On my return today I hoped to have found a line or two from you informing me what decision (if any) was come to at your meeting last Tuesday respecting the result of the survey which you made of this part of the line last Monday week.

I now trouble you with this to enquire how we had better proceed to bring the matter fairly before your Board. It appears to me that as we have already addressed two Memorials (signed by very respectable Inhabitants of this Town and Neighbourhood) as well as a letter to your Chairman and a letter to Mr. Brunel it now only remains for us to appoint a deputation to wait upon and press our interest upon your notice and I shall be glad if you will let me know what will be the best way and fittest time to do so.

We are determined if possible to have Railway communication with the town and if you are not willing to give it us the sooner we know it the better as we shall then at once proceed to open a negotiation with the London and North Western Interest at Banbury who have already made some overtures to us.

Seeing that Chipping Norton is the most important place you will have on your line between Evesham and Oxford (a distance of 36 to 38 miles) our tonnage being about 3,500 Tons annually, I cannot think that you will consult your own interest by letting this town and neighbourhood fall into the hands of your opponents, which it most certainly will if you do not give us a passenger's station at Bleddington Mill. A station at Addlestrop Gate and Shipton Bridge will be of little or no service to us and instead of leaving our interest in the hands of Local Directors, I wish you and a few others of the Directors would visit this town and see what interest we have to offer, or if you can make an appointment with your chairman to receive a deputation we shall be glad to wait upon you at any place or at any time.

Waiting the favour of a reply to this, I am Dear Sir

Yours truly
W. Bliss.

W. Lewis Esq.
P.S. You must bear in mind that we are the connecting link between your line and Banbury, and that there is only 17 miles of rail wanted to connect the Wash with the Bristol Channel or the East and West Coast of this island which I think may ultimately be of great importance."

Although the Directors of the OW&W had not recorded receiving the second Memorial from Chipping Norton, and had clearly not discussed the request from the respectable inhabitants of the area at their previous meeting, they were obliged to take William Bliss's letter seriously, if only because of the explicit threat that Chipping Norton might enter the London and North Western Railway's network. William Bliss's interest in developing a railway link is made clear by his reference to the tonnage (of coal, presumably) that Chipping Norton was consuming, and his implied criticism of "Local Directors" must refer to Robert Beman of Broadwell, who alone had a personal knowledge of the district. Bliss's letter was read and discussed on 5th October, 1847, and duly transcribed into the Company's minute book – an unusual honour – but the official reply was still unhelpful.

"The subject of the site for the Station on the line in neighbourhood of Chipping Norton has been carefully considered, and after personal inspection by the Chairman and Officials of the company the opinion of the board is that the sites fixed upon are the most eligible and proper to meet the wants and the convenience of the district generally."

The opinion of the Board was almost certainly ill-founded and the Directors could have had little idea of the determination and pertinacity of William Bliss. They had enough problems of their own with the local aristocracy and even for them they were not prepared to make any particular concessions. Lord Northwick and Lord Leigh of Adlestrop were putting pressure on the Company to make special provisions for their respective estates. Lord Northwick and Lord Redesdale were demanding a station on the Paxford Road, with a promise that one train each way every day would stop there. Lord Leigh of Adlestrop Park insisted that, on a signal, first class trains should stop at Adlestrop and take up and set down passengers for Adlestrop House. By March 1848 the Company was not to be pressurised into making such provisions. They record that Lord Leigh's "proposal is so objectionable that it cannot be conceded" (20th March, 1848).

However, by 1848, the OW&W was no longer in a position to consider expansion and the Company was finding itself hard pressed to maintain even the nominal construction work that still continued. The failure of the OW&W to complete the construction of the line must have dampened the ardour of William Bliss, but had not quenched his enthusiasm for the new form of transport. Indeed, in 1851 he was "building a power loom shed and carding room with machinery driven by a steam engine of the old beam type" in the Upper Mill, and therefore his need for a plentiful supply of cheap coal was increasing.

In April 1852, the OW&W once again had their construction work under way and the line from Worcester to Evesham was almost completed. Once again, Chipping Norton approached the Company with a third Memorial, which appears to have been disregarded. On May 1st, 1852, the line to Evesham was opened, and the *Illustrated London News* devoted a full page article to the event with three pictures giving the artist's impressions, particularly of the open-air junketings in Evesham market place, where the banner enjoining the assembled public to "Eat, Drink and be Merry" may well have carried an ominous message to the representatives of the Company. At the end of 1852 yet another Memorial from Chipping Norton was delivered to the Company.

The line to Oxford was at last opened in May 1853. Stations on the route were decorated with flowers, flags and evergreens to welcome the train carrying representatives of the Company on the first journey along the whole length of the line. Crowds turned out on the stations, and the local bands appeared, inevitably playing "See the Conquering Hero Comes" despite the steady downpour of drenching rain that continued all day. But there was no particular rejoicing at Chipping Norton; there was still no station, nor even a halt at Bledington Mill, and there was no proposal to construct a rail link with the town. At this point, it may be well to observe that the ambitions of William Bliss had moved beyond merely securing a station on the OW&W line. The postscript to his letter in 1847 makes clear that he was already thinking in terms of a rail link between the OW&W in the neighbourhood of Chipping Norton, and the LNWR at Banbury. He now involved another leading manufacturer in the town in his project, Mr. Robert Hitchman of Hitchman's Breweries, founded in 1796. William Bliss and Robert Hitchman politely attributed to each other the initiative in finally securing permission to construct the line, but the credit must surely have been due to Bliss.

Early in 1851 Chipping Norton, and Bliss in particular, must have been alarmed by a new development in local railway projects. On April 21st, 1851, an 'Important Railway Meeting', as the *Banbury Guardian* described it, was held at the Red Lion at Banbury. The purpose of the meeting was to promote a line westwards to link Banbury with the Oxford, Worcester and Wolverhampton line now under construction. Proposals for the new route were put forward and a map was on display for all to examine. It has not yet proved possible to identify the proposed railway with certainty, but the indications given in the *Banbury Guardian* all point to the South Wales and Northamptonshire Junction Railway, whose plans were deposited in 1853. This railway followed a route nineteen miles long, linking Banbury with the Oxford, Worcester and Wolverhampton line, then under construction near Moreton-in-Marsh. The selected route ran further north than the Chipping Norton line which was ultimately constructed many years later, passing through North Newington, Broughton and Tadmarton, to reach the valley of the upper Stour near Sibford Ferris. On paper, this route gave much more sensible gradients and brought the railway to within a couple of miles of Shipston-on-Stour before bearing south-west to link with the Worcester line about a mile north of Moreton-in-Marsh. The advantage of this railway for Shipston was specially emphasised at the Banbury meeting, at which Lord Duncan, who represented the Shipston interest, had been elected chairman. The isolation of Shipston was mournfully described by the speakers and it was pointed out that letters and news from London reached Edinburgh sooner than they reached Shipston.

Many other advantages were also put forward, which can be roughly classified into two categories. In the first case, the east-west route proposed would bring Banbury into direct touch with the manufacturing districts of the north and west, and also with the mineral district of South Wales. This would enable coal to be transported more cheaply from the Welsh mining districts and statistics were quoted of the fall in the price of coal in Oxford since the construction of the railway there, although these statistics were apparently challenged by someone present who asked to know whether they were for coal of the same quality. In particular, anthracite was cited as a fuel in great demand in the Banbury area, which could be imported more easily by rail.

The other chief consideration at the meeting was agriculture. The proposed railway would provide an opportunity for the farmers of the Stour valley to bring their produce into Banbury market, no doubt to the disadvantage of the Shipston market. But the particular attraction offered to the farmers of Banbury and Buckinghamshire was the possibility of bringing the coveted Herefordshire cattle direct by rail. The Herefordshire breed had just recently become of great importance to beef farmers. Developed in the border lands of Hereford and Monmouth in the 1840s, the white-faced Herefordshire cattle were an immediate success. The repeal of the Corn Laws in 1846 drove arable farmers to reconsider their farming policy and to turn to grazing, and those on the rich grazing lands of the Midlands soon began to look to the new breed as a source of wealth. But in the days before the construction of railways, cattle intended for slaughter were driven on the hoof from the upland breeding grounds to the Midlands, where they were fattened, and then again to the cattle markets of London and the Black Country. Needless to say, the long journey neither improved the quality of the beef, nor reduced the cost of the cattle. It was a great inducement for the Midland farmers centred on the great cattle market of Banbury, therefore, to agitate for a new east-west railway to be constructed. (Strange to think that today, 125 years later, Banbury cattle market is the largest in the Kingdom, albeit served by juggernaut road vehicles.)

The first project for an east-west route was the 'East & West of England Junction Railway', projected and surveyed in 1845. This railway was designed to join the (as yet unbuilt) OW&W line just north of the Bruern Crossing, but soon picked up the line later used by the Chipping Norton branch. The plans for this railway were deposited with the Clerk of the Peace for Oxfordshire, but for reasons unrecorded the project was never developed. The proposals that were being considered at the Banbury Meeting in 1851 clearly relate to a different project; a railway link between Banbury and the OW&W which cut out Chipping Norton entirely. This had first been proposed in 1845 as the 'Northampton, Banbury and Cheltenham Railway', and was now being revived under the new name of 'South Wales and Northamptonshire Junction Railway'. The intention of constructing a direct link between the South Midlands and the coal and cattle area of South Wales and the Border was evident. Equally evident was the geography of the new line which followed the upper valley of the Sor brook westwards from Banbury to Swalcliffe, cut across the narrow valley at Sibford Ferris and joined the valley of the Stour at the extreme northern tip of the parish of Hook Norton. The route thence ran westwards to join the OW&W line a couple of miles north of Moreton-in-Marsh. This route would have brought the line within two miles of Shipston-on-Stour, whence it derived its greatest support; it would also have effectively isolated Chipping Norton. Any east-west route to be constructed from Banbury to the OW&W line must lead necessarily to commercial rivalry between Chipping Norton and Shipston. Messrs. Bliss and Hitchman would have to move fast if Chipping Norton was not to become an industrial backwater.

The new approach was made in about 1853 when William Bliss and Mr. Wilkins of Chipping Norton led a deputation to the OW&W to request a station at Bledington. This request was again refused and the company sent representatives to Chipping Norton to explain the reasons for their decision. At this point, Bliss, Hitchman and the 'Respectable Inhabitants' of Chipping Norton determined to undertake the work themselves. The opportunity for this lay in the unexpected decision of Sir Morton Peto, the railway contractor, to build and to help finance the line himself.

Sir Samuel Morton Peto, Bart, (another prominent Baptist!) was born at Woking in 1809, and together with another nephew, one Grissel, inherited his uncle's contracting business in 1830. This redoubtable pair were responsible for the building of many famous London landmarks such as The Lyceum, The Reform Club and Nelson's Column. Later, Edward Ledd Betts joined Peto and between 1846 and 1872 their achievements were world-wide, including not only the South Eastern Railway, the LC&D Railway, and the LTS Railway, but abroad, the Grand Trunk Railway of Canada and a military railway in the Crimea which earned him a baronetcy in 1855.

Thus it was then, when these two eminent Baptists, Peto and Bliss, finally came together, the matter of the Chipping Norton line was raised, and such must have been William Bliss's eloquence that Peto decided not only to build the line but also to risk £14,000 of his own private fortune to the enterprise.

The estimate for the branch was for a total of £26,000 and the balance of £12,000 was made up by the inhabitants of Chipping Norton and district, the subscription list headed of course by none other than William Bliss.

One must add to this pair of champions two other names which made the line possible: one was a local landowner Mr. J.H. Langston, M.P., who not only owned most of the land upon which the railway was to be built, but who also sold the property at a reasonable price and without any of the more usual costly 'conditions of sale'; the other was William Rolls who, as secretary to the committee of the 'Chipping Norton' railway, successfully ironed out the many legal and pecuniary difficulties which always beset such an undertaking.

Thus it came to pass, in September of 1854, Messrs. Peto & Bett, contractors, with John Fowler as the engineer, commenced work on a single line of track which left the Oxford, Worcester and Wolverhampton's main line at a point to be known as 'Chipping Norton Junction'. This intersection was situated half-way between Adlestrop and Shipton station, and in the beginning consisted only of a single house selling tickets. Two signal boxes were provided, one at the junction serving the main and branch lines and also one at Chipping Norton itself. The track was to the 4' 8½" gauge from its inception and laid with 65 lb. double-headed rail on cross sleepers. A small halt was erected close by the village of Churchill, but called Sarsden in deference to a whim of J.H. Langston, another important landowner who lived at Sarsden House. So, in the autumn of 1854, approximately 400 'navvies' descended on Chipping Norton, much to the dismay of the civil authorities and the delight of the local maidens, and by working day and night, completed the 4½ miles long branch by Whit Monday 1855, keeping within the estimated cost of £26,000, an event unheard of on the Oxford, Worcester and Wolverhampton Railway which undertook to work the line on a consideration of 50% of the revenue earned! *(See Map 2 of 1855.)*

As usual, the opening called for a celebration dinner, the press report of which is given on page 125.

I have sketched in this history of the Chipping Norton branch perhaps more lavishly than necessary in such a small work, which deals with the whole Banbury-Cheltenham line, but I feel that this first section, opened in 1855, was so obviously the beginning of the whole eventual east-west branch, that, but for the dogged perseverance of William Bliss, coupled with the confidence and finances of Sir Morton Peto, the whole venture would surely have ended at Bledington Mill.

Perhaps I can finalize the Chipping Norton branch by mentioning two of the early engines which operated the line, the timetable, and the fares.

Firstly the engines. There were two special little 2-2-2 well tanks, made by R. Stephenson and Co. and which came from the Henwick-Malvern Link line to work both the 'Chippy' branch and also the 'Bourton Line' in 1859. These little tanks, nos. 52 and 54, had outside cylinders, large American style cabs and ornamented domes. No. 52 having the name *Ben Jonson,* it was not long before no. 54 became known as *Mrs Jonson. (See No. 1 Page 137 for diagram.)* These engines worked on the branches until 1877, being scrapped twelve months later.

As for their service, 'Bradshaw' of 1855 gives three trains, weekdays only to Chipping Norton Junction, 8.30 am., 11.10 am and 6.00 pm, returning to Chipping Norton at 9.25 am, 12.25 pm and 7.50 pm.

Fares were 5*s.* 7*d.* 1st class and 4*s.* 4*d.* 2nd class, from Oxford to Chipping Norton. Chipping Norton Junction to Chipping Norton, 10*d.* 1st class and 9*d.* 2nd class.

In 1859, the Oxford, Worcester and Wolverhampton Railway, realizing at last, no doubt, that the little line was financially sound, purchased it on a guarantee of 4%, and it was in this same year, that another link in the chain was forged. Parliament passed a Bill for a six mile branch, running westwards this time, again from Chipping Norton Junction, through Stow-on-the-Wold (or at least a station one mile south of the village), to Bourton-on-the-Water. One year later, the West Midland Railway absorbed the OW&W Railway and in so doing took over the responsibility for working and maintaining the new 'Bourton-on-the-Water Railway'. Peto again was the contractor for this new branch line and only three years after the Act was passed

Map 2

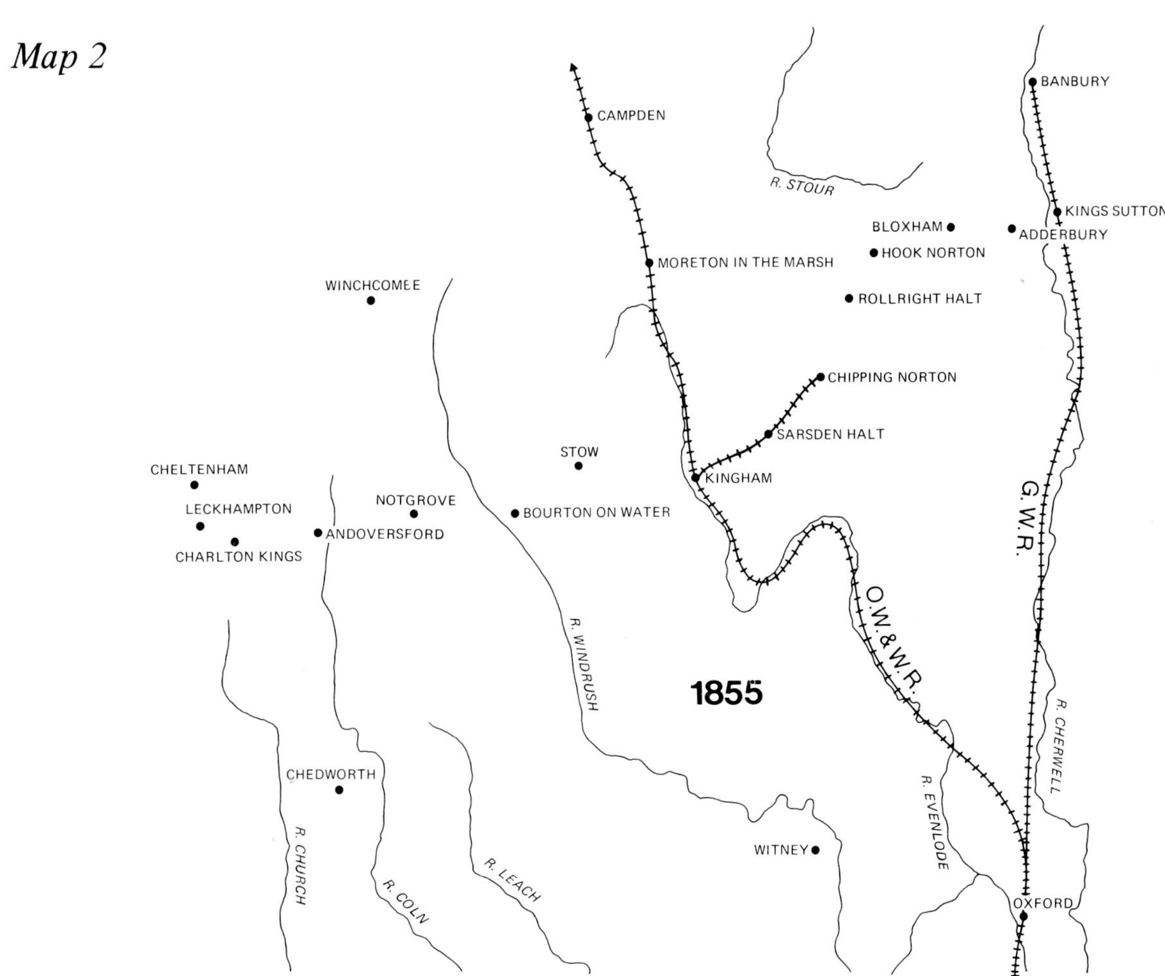

Map 3

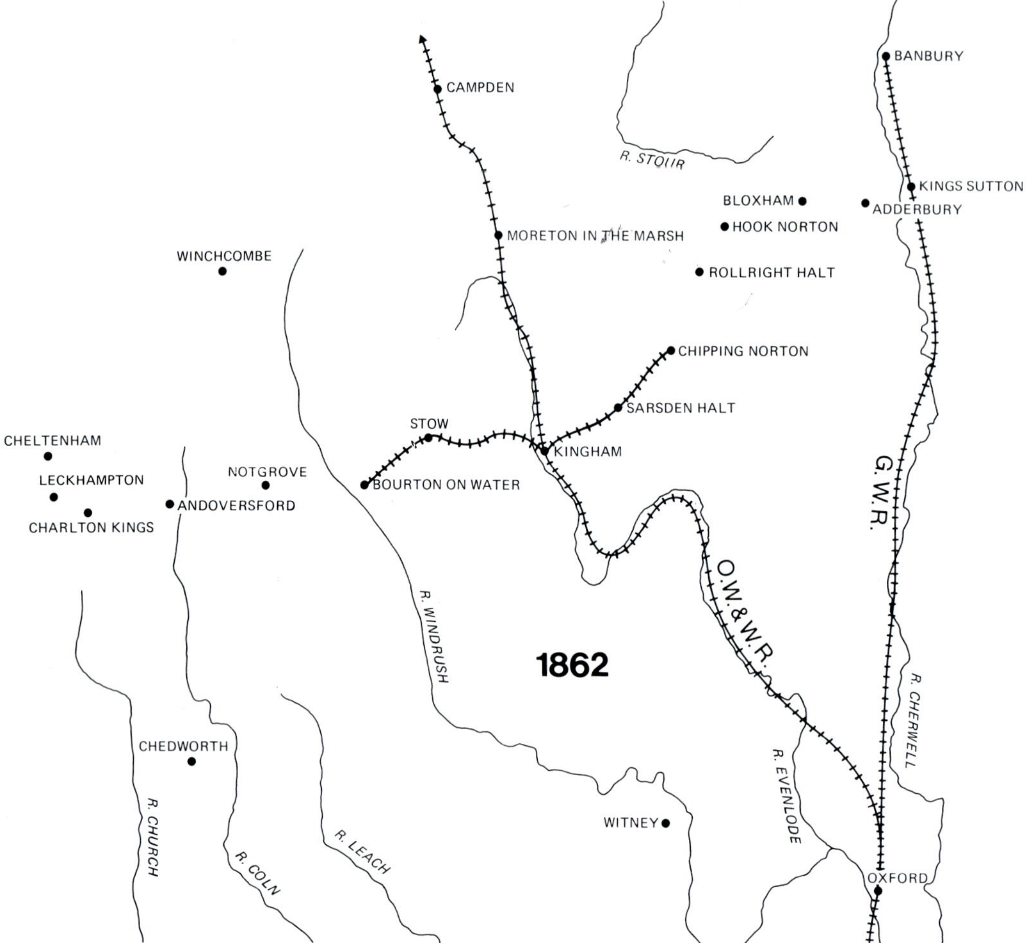

traffic started to run from Chipping Norton Junction to Bourton on March 1st, 1862, with four trains daily each way, even though the stations at both Stow and Bourton were not completed until 1863. *(See Map 3 of 1862.)*

Plans were also laid for a spur off the branch at Chipping Norton Junction towards Honeybourne, so that through working could operate between Bourton and Evesham, but this scheme was not proceeded with. The next proposal of note came in 1861, when the 'East Gloucestershire Railway' was promoted in the Cheltenham area. This line was intended to run from Cheltenham to Faringdon, with a branch from Fairford to Witney making an end-on connection there, and so gaining access to Oxford and London!

However, this scheme was altered slightly, the EG Railway coming to an understanding with the joint MR/GWR that the branch towards Witney would be changed for a similar line, but running from Andoversford to Bourton-on-the-Water.

John Fowler and James Burke prepared the plans for this new line and added a westerly spur towards Gloucester. It was to be of mixed gauge again as far as Andoversford, but the scheme, being opposed by the shareholders of the GWR was abandoned in 1863.

With this proposal's demise, up sprang another to take its place in 1864. This was the 'Gloucester, Cheltenham and Oxford Direct Railway', which was incorporated to construct a line of route from Cheltenham to Witney direct, via Andoversford, Northleach and Burford.

Meantime over in the east, things were also moving, for in 1864 schemes were formulated for the Banbury-Chipping Norton Railway area. One was by John Fowler and Edward Wilson and was very similar to the final route laid down, except that it passed through the village of Swerford, instead of Hook Norton, and the junction off the GWR main line was planned to be one mile nearer Banbury than Kings Sutton. Another plan was to run from Blockley on the West Midland, along the valley of the Stour, and link up, by means of a triangular junction with the LNWR at Banbury. This scheme was put forward by Chas. Liddell and John Collister. Yet another project was the 'Chipping Norton and East and West Joint Railway' put forward by James Burke, who suggested running on the Sibford side of Hook Norton and crossing the GWR at Banbury to pass up between the latter and the LNWR, before joining the East and West Joint Railway (Stratford and Midland Junction) near Moreton Pinkney. One more idea was that put out by James Burke also, backed by Edward Wilson, for the 'Bourton-Chipping Norton and Banbury Railway', making a four-way connection at Kingham for running in every direction, on and off the West Midland, and connecting eventually with both GWR and LNWR at Banbury.

However, things died down somewhat, in the late sixties, owing to another national financial crisis and all four promotions proved fruitless, until, in the year 1871, a really major extension from the Northampton-Banbury line (LNWR) was proposed, to run from Banbury to Ross-on-Wye via Blockley! Too ambitious, this scheme was shortened in 1873 to be just 'Banbury-Blockley Railway', but it came to nought as with so many of the other proposals. The final plan, and the one to which the line was built, was prepared by Edward Wilson, which included triangular junctions at both Cheltenham and Kings Sutton originally, but these were not proceeded with, although the Hatherley curve in the west did eventually take shape in 1906. In 1874 Wilson was given the go-ahead for the 'Banbury and Cheltenham Direct Railway', and instructed to purchase land for the building of stations at Cheltenham, Andoversford, Salperton, Hook Norton, Bloxham and Adderbury and to enlarge and improve the existing Bourton and Chipping Norton stations. £35,000 was allotted for the purpose of constructing these buildings, but two changes were made in the proposal, one being that Salperton site was moved to Aylworth Down, and subsequently became Notgrove, and the other was the deferment of the building of Adderbury, as it was considered to be so close to Kings Sutton as to be of little use. However, as we now know, the growth of the iron ore quarries in this eastern area finally swayed the balance and Adderbury was given a small station.

Among the many proposals for the line in 1875, was one that considered making Leckhampton Road, the station for Cheltenham, but at that time it was away from the town and this was decided against. (Later the name was changed to Cheltenham South and Leckhampton, for the sole purpose of allowing the 'Welsh Express' to pick up and set down at Cheltenham.)

The increase and importance of the iron ore traffic at the eastern end of the branch, added a clause on the plans that at least two long sidings and passing loops were to be provided at every station for the purpose of handling this potential traffic. Also, in the summer of 1875, it was decided to provide stations at Edward's Lime Kiln, Charlton Kings and Great Rollright, but of these three, only Charlton Kings became a station as such, and later Rollright was served by a small halt, as were Sarsden and Milton.

The grandiose object of the prospectus for the 'Banbury and Cheltenham Direct Railway' was to connect London, the Midlands, and the eastern county districts, by a shorter and more direct route, with the South Wales coalfield and the West of England. The main support for the line was expected to come from the transportation of iron ore to Wales to the tune of 10,000 tons daily, and the GWR had already agreed to work the line in perpetuity.

However, all this planning was slightly optimistic and again national unstability in 1878 caused a suspension of building. When restarted in the autumn of 1879, priority was given to the western section Bourton to Cheltenham, and when the Lansdowne Junction was connected through running could commence from Cheltenham to Oxford. The service was inaugurated on June 1st, 1881. *(See Map 4 of 1881.)*

Map 4

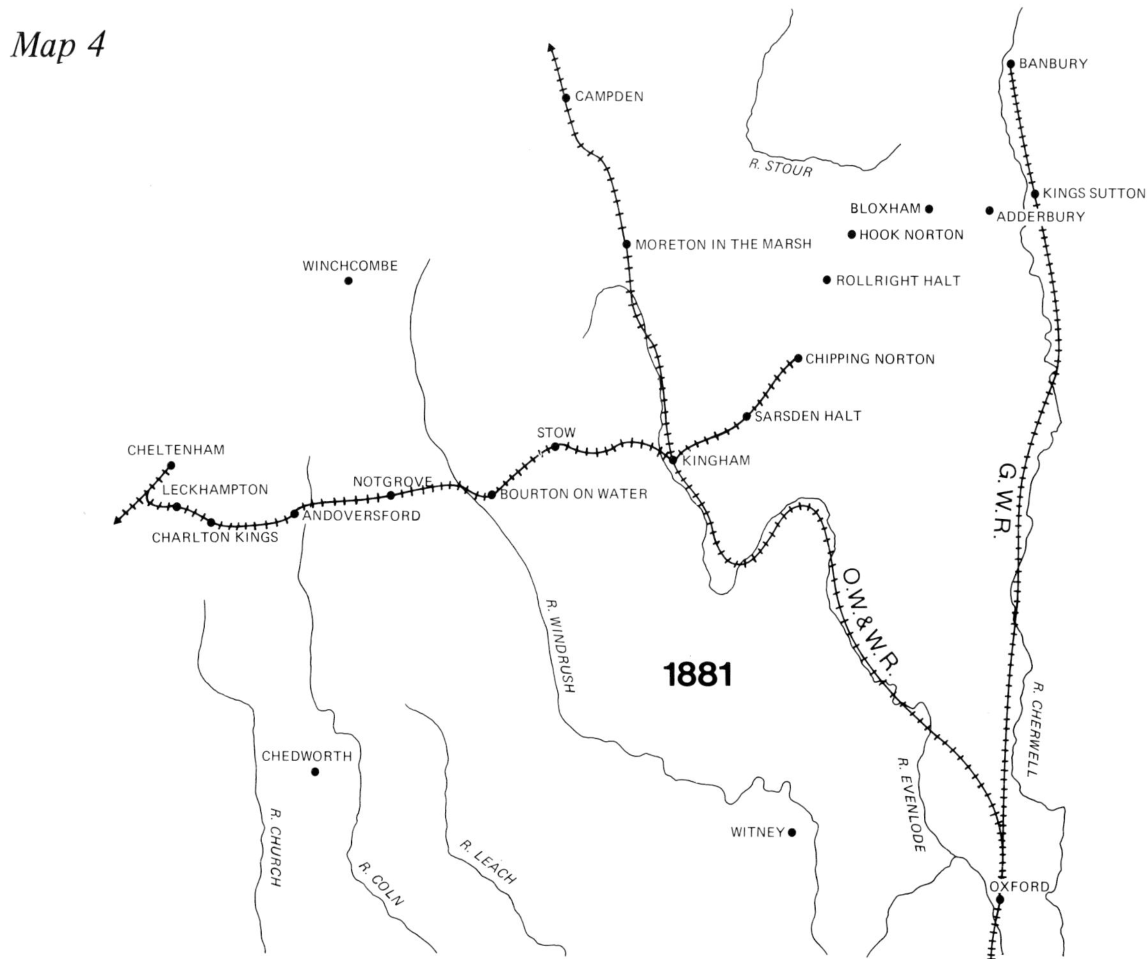

Map 5

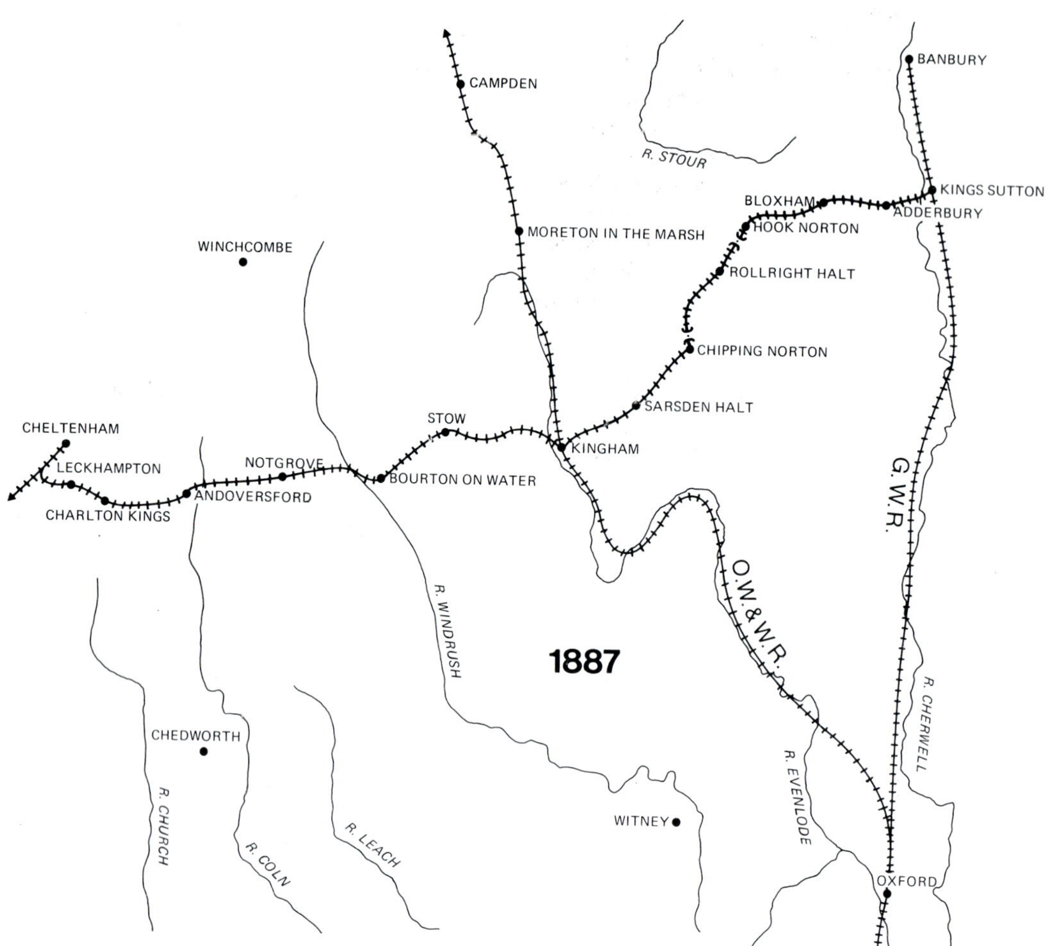

Here, then, was our Banbury-Cheltenham line, still not complete, but three of the five phases in place:

Chipping Norton Junction to Chipping Norton station in 1855

Chipping Norton Junction to Bourton station in 1862

Cheltenham to Bourton via Andoversford in 1881

Meantime, work was proceeding apace on the eastern section, Chipping Norton-Banbury. A tunnel and two viaducts were built at Hook Norton at an additional cost of £25,000, which brought the line closer to the village and, of course, nearer to the iron ore workings. Also, plans were formulated in 1877 for extra spurs at Chipping Norton Junction, to allow through working from the east branch to the west branch. Finally, work was completed on the Kings Sutton-Chipping Norton stretch and this part was officially opened on April 6th, 1887. *(See Map 5 of 1887.)* At last it was possible to travel from Banbury to Cheltenham, although it still meant a change (or a reversal) at Chipping Norton Junction. More traffic was channelled on to the western end in 1891 when the Midland and South Western Junction Railway opened its line from Cirencester to Andoversford, and obtained running powers over the branch to Cheltenham, which was made double track in 1900. Finally, a steel girder bridge was erected in 1906 over the Oxford-Worcester line at Kingham, and a double track cut-off enabled complete through working to operate from Banbury to Cheltenham and so made possible the daily one-each-way South Wales-Newcastle Express (except Sundays).

Fig 1

Along the route

The Banbury station of my memories, was an old Brunel affair with the typical all-over wooden roof, built originally for the broad gauge, and with a complete disregard for travellers' comforts. I knew it as a child as a place for watching the trains, as a youth when it became the venue for my first employment, and I was there when it was pulled down, to make way for the concrete structure that now answers to the name Banbury.

Draughty and old-fashioned it certainly was and yet I remember it with affection. There were only two through platform faces, one on each of the Up and Down main lines, with a bay at the north end of the Down line, and two bays on the Up side, one at the north end and one at the south end of the station. It was from this latter bay that the Auto car train for Kingham started out.

Looking north towards Birmingham, Figure 1 shows the old station. On the left is the signboard telling passengers to 'Change here for the Banbury and Cheltenham Line'. Just beyond the 'Banbury' sign, is the old porter's room, then comes the station building proper, almost at the end of its days. Most of the glazing has gone, and the main timbers are sagging sadly. Inside, and over the tracks, one can just see the lattice footbridge which linked the Down platform to the Up. The station entrance was to the left of the picture, whilst on the right were four goods lines linking Banbury North End Yard to Banbury South and the Loco Sheds.

Figure 2 (overleaf) shows the station frontage, still looking north but taken from the Goods Shed road. The hand winch, centre right, was for pulling road vehicles off wagons standing in the goods dock, extreme right. The reason for that massive telegraph pole in the centre of the picture, is that Banbury was a central point on the telegraph system of the railway and just behind the yard gate was situated the telegraph office, where at one time a senior clerk, two juniors and a messenger laboured. (I was one of the messengers in 1929!) All wires and telegrams were transmitted on the single needle principle, there being four such machines in the Banbury office as well as telephone switchboards, not only to the GPO but to many of the principal stations on the Great Western, and even one on to the LNER.

Figure 3 is included solely because it shows the small wagon turntable which used to exist at the south end of the Down platform. It can just be seen in front of the coal wagon, on the extreme left. The photograph was taken from the staging of a tea warehouse, which occupied a site in the goods yard.

Fig 2

Fig 3

Fig 4

Figure 4 shows the Down side of Banbury station in detail from the Leamington end. Starting from the right is the Refreshment Room, with the hamper outside for soiled cups and saucers taken out of the trains. Next is the bookstall on the left, which in my time was Wymans Ltd. Next to that is the exit for parcels and mail traffic, and which also led to the Stationmaster's office (behind the bookstall). On the left was the parcels office manned continuously in those days. Just to the left of the bicycle was the label rack, complete with paste pot, for luggage labels to be stuck on passengers' trunks, etc., by porters. Under the bridge was a slot of a room called the Waiting Room, adjacent to the main passenger entrance.

Next came the Telegraph Office mentioned before; then the Ladies' Room, staffed always by an elderly lady, usually a railway widow, who kept this sanctuary spotless and strictly sacrosanct to the female sex. Finally the 'Gents' and Porters' Room outside the partition.

Looking back south, Figure 5 shows No. 2931, the passenger Pilot, standing in the Down platform on a summer midday morning. You may ask how I can tell this, but the answer is in that red board sticking out at right angles by the engine's cab, stating 'Leicester, York and Newcastle Express'. This train was due into Banbury at 12.44 pm, therefore the time must be approximately 12.15 pm. This cross-country express (one in each direction every weekday) was the 7.40 am Swansea which, after leaving Gloucester, took the Hatherley curve and reached Banbury via Andoversford and Chipping Norton, but more of this train later.

Fig 5

Official track Plan of the Great Western and London Midland and Scottish stations at Banbury.

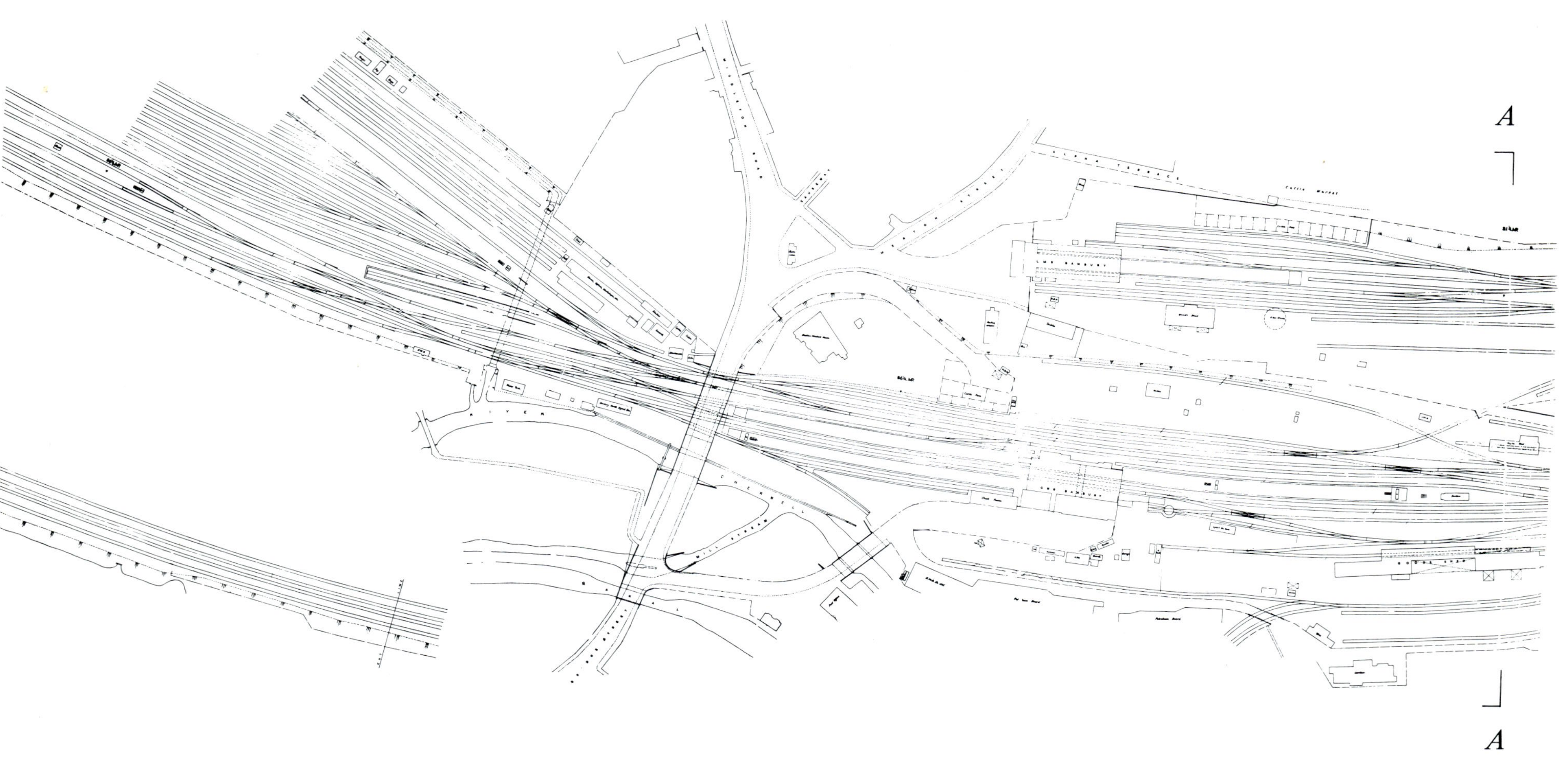

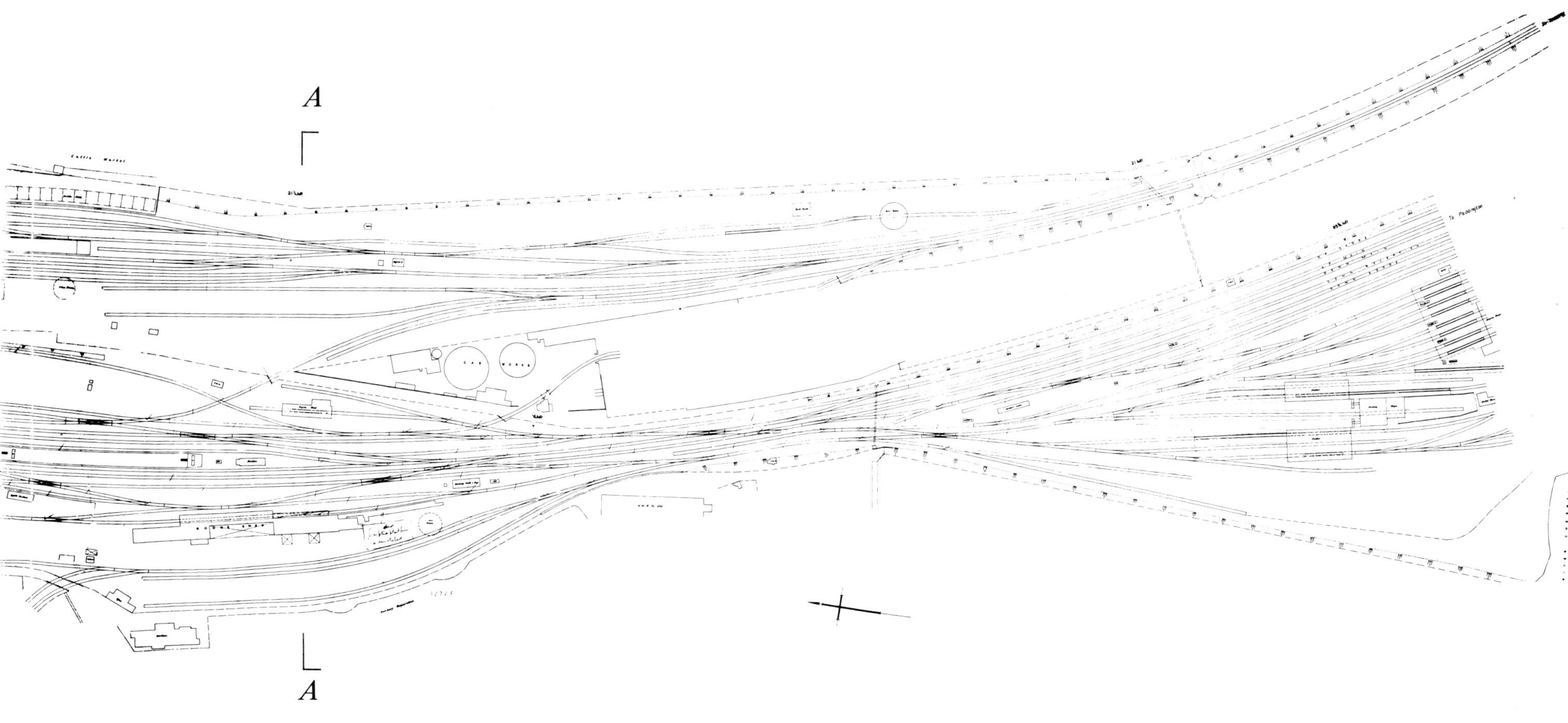

Official Plan continued.

Fig 6

Figure 6 shows the Up side of Banbury station with many interesting advertisements still in place. In the background is Platform 3 from which passengers travelling south joined their trains. Platform 5 was the Up bay at the north end and into which the LNER motor trains from Woodford terminated, whilst at the opposite end Platform 4 can just be seen, from where the local shuttle service, Banbury-Kingham started.

Several points of interest appear here. Extreme left is the drinking water can, which had to be filled and returned daily to the lady in charge of Wormleighton Crossing, as there was no water there. Behind the can is the rack in which coach blank doors were stored on edge, and behind the glazed window was a stock of GW tail lamps, for every LNER train that came in not only had its engine and train crew changed, but also the NE lamps came off and a proper Great Western pattern was substituted.As a lad this was another of my jobs! The station clock can just be seen to the right of the second gas lamp.

But enough of Banbury, let's catch the 'Chippy car' from the Up bay and commence our journey. Figure 7 is a good illustration of the actual unit, engine No. 1155 and car No. 11 seen at Kings Sutton.

Leaving Banbury station we join the main line and pass the South Box on the right with the Gas works on the left. The extensive locomotive depot was on the right hand of the track here.

Four tracks now head south to Astrop Sidings. Up and Down main lines in the centre and a goods running loop on each side of the main lines. Two miles from Banbury, the two long loops, which often held four and five goods trains, converge and rejoin the main line. This was the site of the first of many ironstone workings around this area and I can just remember the kilns and sidings being in place here. The signal box here is called 'Astrop Sidings' after the sidings which connected off the main line to the east. The Astrop ironstone mines were situated approximately one mile to the north of King's Sutton and on the left coming from Banbury. The railway sidings were laid in the cutting that still exists today, and five calcining kilns were erected between these sidings and the rock face of the cutting. As the mineral tramway was on the top of the bank, this natural difference in levels enabled the ore to be tipped straight into the tops of the kilns. The kilns were for drying ore. Coal and ore was loaded into these 80 foot high kilns and fired, the resultant dried ore dropping out of chutes at the bottom of

Map 6

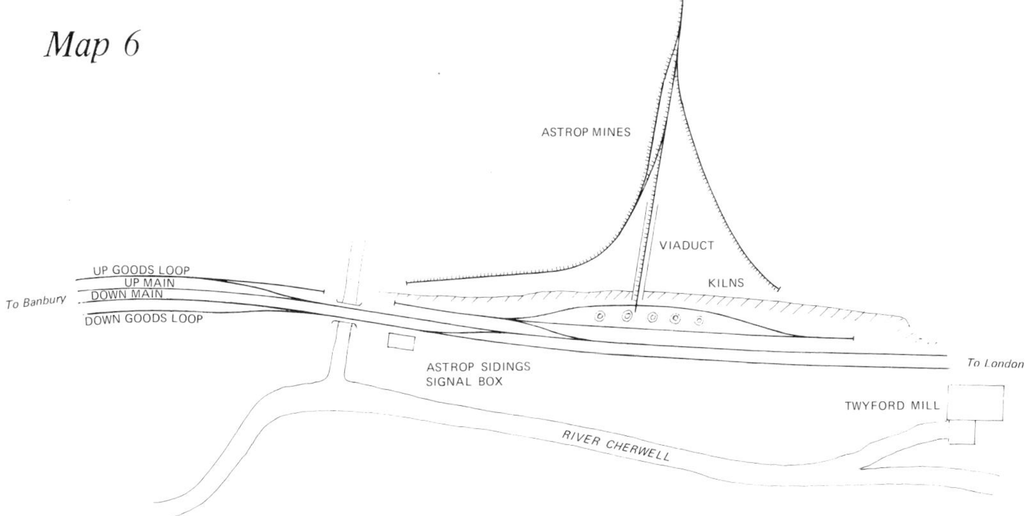

the kiln into waiting standard gauge wagons. Work started here in 1897 and continued until 1920, when labour troubles and poor quality ore combined to close the pits and all working ceased in 1925. See the sketch map for details.

Before leaving Astrop, I must mention one tragic accident that happened here. On the Up loop, at the exit, was a piece of throw off track, which ended on the banks of a stream which passed under the main lines. In the early thirties a goods train got out of control coming up the loop and overran the points, the engine ran off the end of the rails, down into the stream and up the other side. The jack-knifing of the engine and tender killed the driver and fireman in a horrible fashion.

However, let's leave Astrop, and passing Twyford Flour Mills on the right, we run through the water meadows to King's Sutton. This little station used to be the junction where the Chipping Norton branch swung off to the right, leaving the main line to carry on towards Aynho, Oxford and London.

On leaving school and joining the Great Western Railway at the tender age of fourteen years, King's Sutton was my first experience of railway work. As a lad my first job was to go on my hands and knees and dig out the weeds between the platform slabs; a lowly but essential task this, because my overlord, Mr. Gardner the Station Master, always entered Kings Sutton in the station gardens competition and indeed often won the first prize. Hence, no weed dare show its timid face, otherwise 'Young Jim' caught it in the neck, or rather on the bottom with a well placed boot!

It is perhaps not generally known that the little village of King's Sutton has a spring of spa water. This railed-in enclosure of brine issue, was, and perhaps still is, situated in a meadow close by the station Up home signal, and in my time was known colloquially as 'Bogwater'. The liquid tasted like the spa water of Leamington Spa, and was supposed to be good for rheumatism. However, it was never in great demand!

As will be seen from the track plan of the station, the branch swung right just outside the signal box, and continued as double track right through to Adderbury. The curvature immediately leaving the main line was so severe it needed a continuous check rail on the inside of both tracks. Leaving the junction, the twin tracks were carried on a low red brick viaduct first over the River Cherwell and then over the Oxford canal. When passing over the river, if one looked south, it was possible to see the engine pump house on the banks of the river, which was in daily use pumping water to the large balance tank for the Aynho water troughs, situated at Nell Bridge. This pump house and the whole troughs installation were maintained and staffed by the Locomotive Department at Banbury.

Kings Sutton

Fig 7

Fig 8

Figure 8 shows another example of the engine and trailer unit which was used for the Banbury-Kingham service. This picture of engine No. 524, one of the '517' class with trailer car No. 33 and the location is just north of King's Sutton station.

I have managed to secure seven photographs to illustrate King's Sutton station. In Figure 9, 'Bulldog' class engine No. 3338 *Swift* is seen with an Up Paddington express of the 1920's. Note the 'slip' coach at the rear, being returned to London after having slipped off a Down express. This view was taken looking north towards the station building from the Down refuge siding.

From the same spot, but this time looking south, Figure 10 shows Dean Goods, No. 2552, with the local stopping goods train just passing King's Sutton signal box. Notice the bracket signal in front of the farm-track bridge, which controlled the entrance to the Kingham branch.

Viewed from the signal-box, and looking up the tracks towards London, Figure 11 illustrates the double line junction well and the Banbury-Cheltenham branch can be seen swinging away to the right towards Adderbury.

Map 7

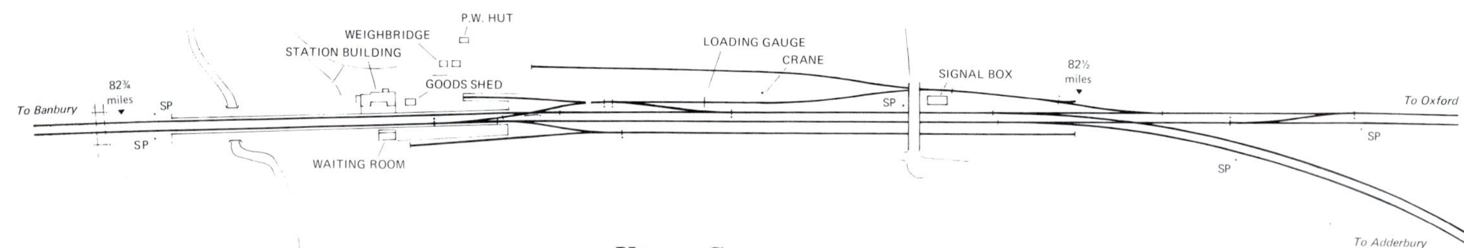

Kings Sutton

Fig 11

Fig 9

Fig 10

Fig 12

In the top picture on this page, we show the 10 am Banbury to Kingham local goods, with the old Armstrong No. 890 just passing the bracket starting signal, which is in the 'off' position for the branch. (Figure 12.) The lower illustration is of the Swansea-Newcastle express just leaving the Cheltenham-Banbury line, at King's Sutton junction. It can be seen that the rolling stock is all of NER ownership, on its way back to the parent company at Banbury Junction. (Figure 13.)

Fig 13

Fig 14

The large photograph on this page (Figure 14) is of trailer car No. 11 in charge of No. 5114, one of the large Prairie tanks. This was unusual, as the service was normally worked by the '517' 0-4-0 Tank engines; obviously the roster had been upset on this occasion. The small picture shows the style and layout of Kings Sutton station buildings; those tall ornate chimneys were very characteristic of this small village stopping place. The corrugated iron shed on the right was for goods traffic. (Figure 15.)

Fig 15

Fig 16

Fig 17

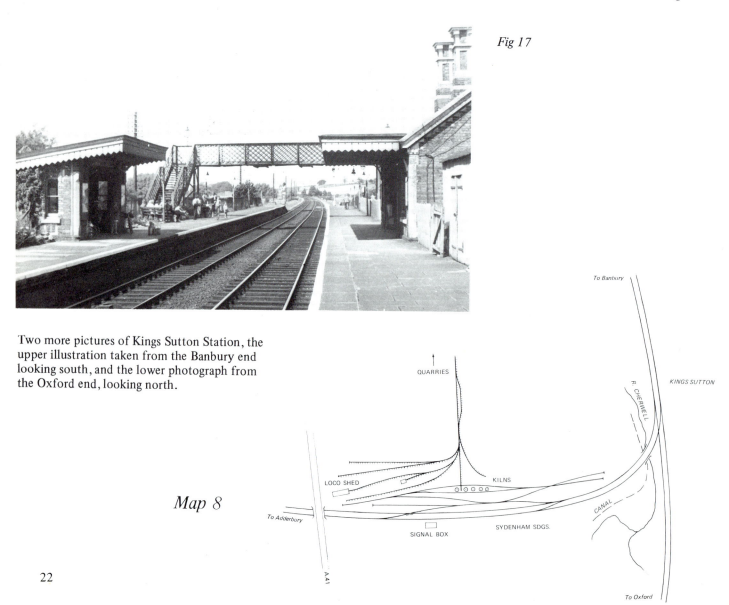

Two more pictures of Kings Sutton Station, the upper illustration taken from the Banbury end looking south, and the lower photograph from the Oxford end, looking north.

To Banbury
QUARRIES
KINGS SUTTON
R. CHERWELL
KILNS
LOCO SHED
CANAL
To Adderbury
SIGNAL BOX
SYDENHAM SDGS.
A.41
To Oxford

Map 8

Just one mile after leaving King's Sutton, we come to Sydenham siding signal box on the left, looking towards Adderbury, and on the right hand side of the track was another extensive iron stone complex. This was the rail head of the East Adderbury Pits, which extended from King's Sutton station in the east to Bo Peep Farm, Adderbury, in the west.

Alongside the railway were erected the usual five kilns but as this site lacked any high ground behind them these kilns had to be filled via a mechanical lift. Steam locomotives were used at the quarry, three small 0-6-0 side tanks in green livery, all made by A. Barclay & Sons, and one 4-6-0T supplied by Hunslet Engine Co. Each engine was named, being *Winifred, Gertrude, The Doll* and *Margaret.* Operations to dig the ore began in 1914 and carried on for twelve years before a general slump in 1926 caused a complete shutdown.

Sketch Map 8 is added to show the extent of the workings and the position of the sidings, etc. I remember the signal box well, as being of typical GW red and blue brick type. As that same small boy, I crept round to Sydenham one day in 1929, and, borrowing the key of the box without permission, entered the empty cabin and started throwing the levers about and ringing block bells, not knowing that this was being recorded in King's Sutton box. I leave my reader to imagine the reception I received when I eventually returned to station duty!

The whole workings at Sydenham, including the kilns, were dismantled by Friswell's of Banbury in 1932 and the site is now occupied by Banbury Buildings of garage fame.

Passing under the A41, the line continued through a shallow cutting on the same curve past Park Farm to Adderbury, and it was this isolated stretch of track which sheltered many royal slumbers. For many years when the Royal Train was in the area and required to remain overnight, it was shunted on to this piece of line, complete with a locomotive to provide steam for train heating, remaining in the peace and quiet of rural Oxfordshire countryside all night long, the branch always closing down after 10 pm. It was supposed to be a secret, of course, and in fact the general public never knew, but the Banbury railwaymen were always aware of the presence.

Adderbury was another station with ironstone connections. Here, the quarry was to the south of the station and was connected to the standard gauge by a 1′ 8″ tramway, worked by one steam loco. The ironstone sidings, which terminated in the station yard on the south side, had a tipping dock and from here the tramway ran due south-west up a steep incline to the quarry face, where the little loco had its shed. The engine concerned was a Manning Wardle 0-4-0T but soon proved unsatisfactory, so a cable working was installed, operated by a stationary steam engine at the top of the incline. These workings came to a close in 1922, although a brief series of operations were reconstituted in 1928 by the Duffield Iron Corporation, but all activities ceased before the Second World War. It is still possible to see where the tramway existed from the main Banbury-Oxford road, at the first cross-roads south of Adderbury village. Map 9 gives the station layout after 1900.

Map 9

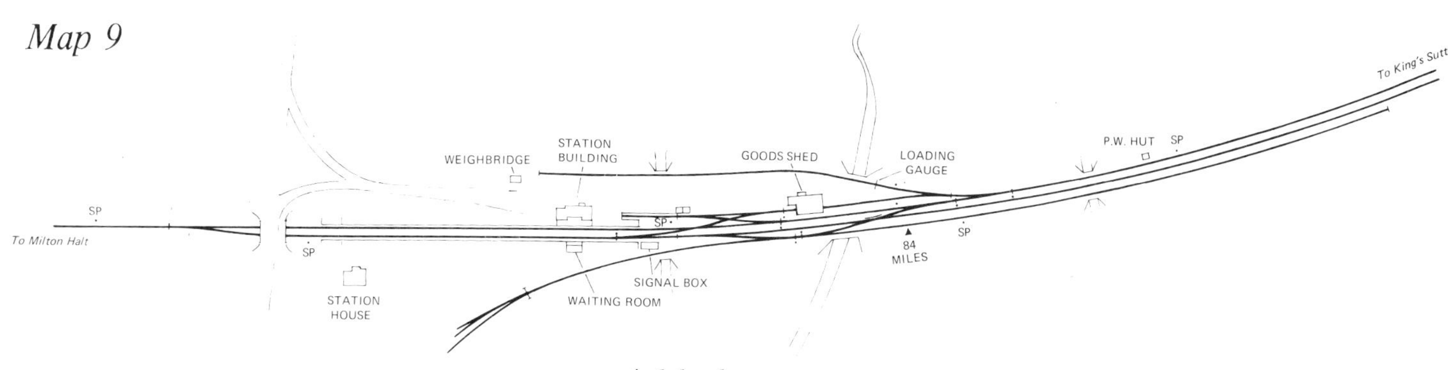

Adderbury

Fig 18

Adderbury

Fig 19

Fig 20

Fig.21

A general view of Adderbury station, looking back towards Banbury, is shown in Figure 18. Both platforms can be seen, with the station buildings somewhat odd at the far end, probably because of the incline of the road approach to the offices.

Figure 20 shows the long descent of the approach road from the Banbury-Oxford A423 to the station and goods yard.

In Figure 21 looking west, the unusual starting signal can be discerned under the overhanging awning, obviously constructed to this pattern for sighting purposes and lack of space. The signal box on the right was taken out bodily when this line was closed and now survives on the private railway system of a steam enthusiast in Oxfordshire!

Figure 21 pictures the small brick shelter which occupied the Up platform, and in the lower photograph both signal cabin and goods shed are seen, together with a good view of the track layout at this point. (Figure 22.)

Fig 22

Fig 23

Fig 24

Fig 25

Three more pictures of Adderbury, all looking westwards to Chipping Norton. Figure 23 shows the private sidings which ran off behind the Up platform to serve Twyfords Seed Co. (formerly E.J. Rank, flour mills). In Figure 24, (taken incidentally from the parapet of the bridge which can be seen at the far end of the platforms in Figure 25) the track can be seen running away past the Down home signal and then the Up advanced starting signal towards Milton. This cutting is now filled in completely.

Leaving Adderbury station, the tracks passed under the main Banbury-Oxford road and then becomes a single line for the first time.

Milton Halt

Another two miles to the west and Milton Halt was reached consisting of a single wooden platform with the usual Great Western 'Pagoda' type corrugated iron building. The Milton importance did not end at the Halt, for there was another extensive ironstone working at Milton Pits, and sidings were duly laid in to handle the ore traffic. The pits were situated east of Bloxham church and were connected to the GWR sidings at Milton by a standard gauge light railway 1½ miles in length. When digging started in 1918, the quarry company took over one of the contractor's steam engines to work the line, a Hunslet 0-6-0 side tank named *Barry* and, together with three wagons, work commenced. Another 0-6-0T loco by Avonside Engine Co. was *Edgar*, which lasted only a short while, and eventually two Peckett 0-6-0 tanks named *Betty* and *Mangot* were bought to replace the two original engines. A real first class loco shed was built down by the railway sidings at Milton Halt. This building had arches at both ends to act as a through shed if needed, but in the event only one end was fitted with doors. (This shed still stands and is in use by the local farmer.) Output continued at Milton until 1924 when the slump set in and thereafter, until 1929, working was spasmodic and closure came in October of 1929. The two engines were

Map 10

Diagram of sidings (not to scale)

To Adderbury

SHELTER

APPROACH PATH

95 MILES

To Bloxham

LOCOMOTIVE SHED

RIVER

MILTON PITS

Milton Halt

taken over by the parent company at Islip ironworks, and some of the equipment found its way to the Oxfordshire Ironstone Co. at Wroxton.

Leaving Milton Halt, the branch continued due west and after one mile entered a deep cutting, passed under two road bridges and a footbridge, before arriving at Bloxham station. During the War this little station saw much traffic, for the RAF had an airfield at Barford, and military personnel often took advantage of the train service to visit Banbury for an evening out. I can remember delivering them to Bloxham on the late special train in 1944/5, many very tipsy and quite a few trying to avoid paying for a ticket! The main station building was on the north side of the station, with a small shelter on the south platform. The signal box was at the end of this same platform and on the other side was a large goods shed.

More ironstone workings, of course, the Bloxham Pits being situated alongside the Tadmarton road, and the workings were joined to the GW sidings by a standard gauge tramway. The rather low grade ore was always loaded by hand straight into the wooden planked 10 ton wagons, although there was a navvy to clear off the subsoil. Work began in 1918 by the Northamptonshire Ironstone Co., followed by the Claycross Co. Operations ceased for a few years in the early twenties recommencing and carrying on spasmodically until 1954, with a five year gap between 1942–47 for the Second World War. Locomotives, for moving the wagons about, were two steam and a petrol electric machine. The steam engines were an 0-6-0ST Peckett, called *Northfield* and a four coupled tank named *Betty*. The other machine was christened *Amos* and was the direct cause of a fatal accident in 1953. Whilst being lifted in the little shed, she slipped off the jacks and fell onto the driver, who later died of his injuries.

Map 11

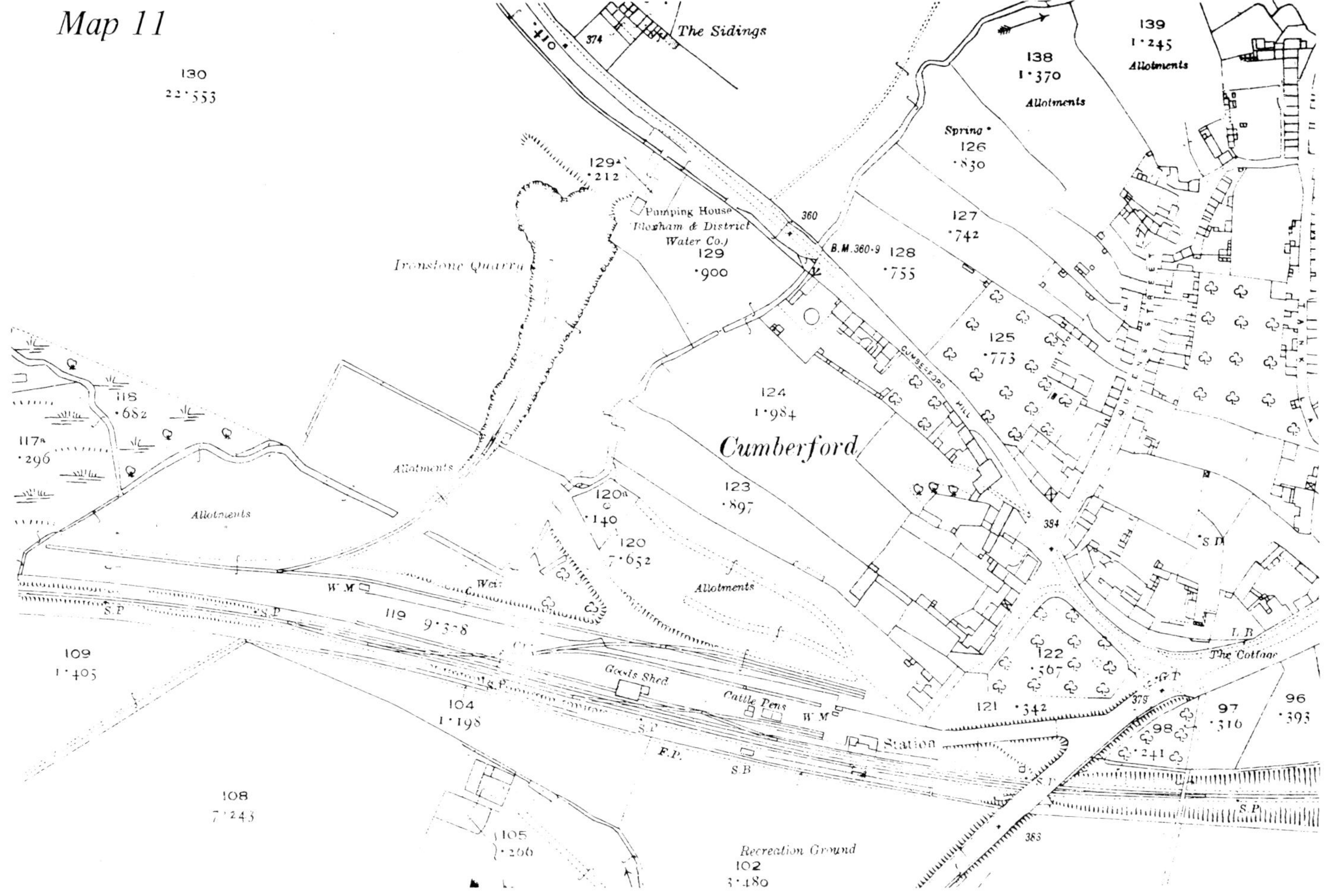

Map 12

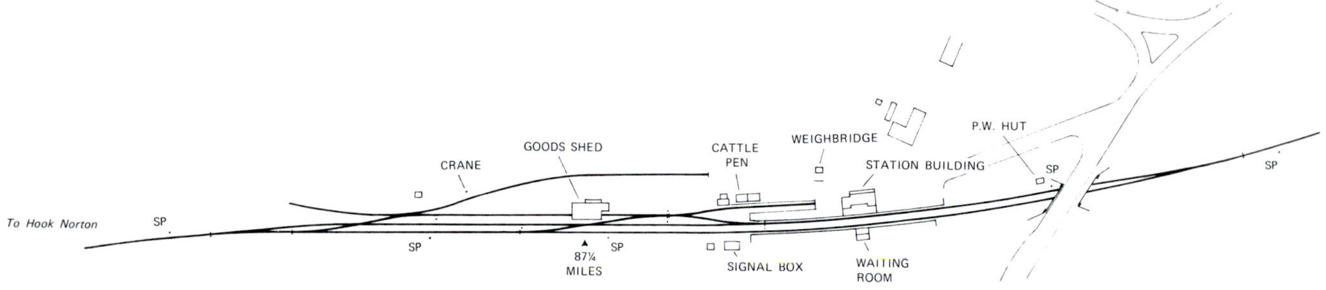

Bloxham

Bloxham

Figure 26 is a general view of the station layout taken from the extreme west of the yard at the Home signal position. It can be seen that the points and the signals are set for a train from Banbury. Figure 27 shows the same scene but closer to the brick built goods shed in the centre. The 5-ton fixed hand crane can be seen on the left and it was directly behind this machine that the siding led off to the open quarries.

The goods shed dominates Figure 28 and one can just distinguish the loading gauge hanging at the entrance to the building.

Fig 26

Fig 27

Fig 28

Fig 29

Fig 30

Closer still to the platforms, Figure 29 depicts the goods yard on the left, the cattle dock just above the ground disc signal, and the signal box on the right hand side alongside the sleepered cabin which contained the motor trolley of the permanent way gang. The west end of the main station building with the station nameboard is seen in Figure 30 and the roof of the Upside shelter can just be distinguished on the right behind the large conifer. Figure 31 is taken from the platform under the awning, still looking towards Banbury. The starting signal can be seen with the 'Shunt' arm fixed halfway down and also the setting down post for receiving the single-line staff.

Fig 31

In this photograph, the single line bears away to the left into the deep cutting towards Milton. The home signal is almost hidden amongst the girders of the arched foot-bridge which carried a right of way.

Fig 32

In Figure 33 the view is westward, towards Hook Norton and is taken from the road bridge at the east end of the station. The barrow crossing shows up clearly in the lower half of the picture. The main station building occupies Figure 34 and was of red brick with slate roof, the wooden canopy extending over the platform. The signal box is of unusual half-brick half-timber style, situated at the western end of the platform. The small corrugated iron hut was the lamp room in which signal and station lamps were trimmed, an excellent vantage point for watching the village football match in the adjacent field! (Figure 35.)

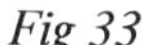

Fig 33

Fig 34

Fig 35

Figure 36 shows the platform shelter on the Up platform at Bloxham.

Fig 36

A fuller view of the signal cabin. Both the set-down and the pick-up posts for the single line token can be discerned in front of the box. (Figure 37.)

The last photograph of Bloxham is in the direction of travel, towards Hook Norton, showing the design and size of the red brick goods shed which used to stand in the yard, all now covered alas with a private housing estate! (Figure 38.)

Fig 37

Fig 38

Time to move on, and turning south-west the line enters a deep cutting, before passing under the single-arch red brick bridge carrying the Golf Course road over the railway. Immediately after the bridge the gradient steepens so severely that at the top of the incline, all goods trains travelling in the opposite direction (downhill) had to stop dead at the summit and draw on down. The guard pinned wagon brakes down, until the driver assessed he had enough brake power in this form and so would whistle for the guard to rejoin the train, which would proceed to the foot of the incline, where the brakes were released. This procedure was always carried out, as we train crews never knew if we were under observation or not. A large hut was situated close by the 'Stop' board and inspectors have been known to lurk therein!

Passing Wigginton village on the left, the next break in the single track came at Brymbo Ironstone Sidings. These were a collection of railway sidings running off to the left, down a steep incline to the 'Brymbo' yard where four kilns were erected for ironstone calcining. **(See Figure 39.)** The history of the ironstone workings here is tied up with the diggings at Hook Norton which opened up first, but as we are travelling west, we must deal with Brymbo first. A large quarrying system started here in 1896, first to the south of the line and then continued to the north and west in what was 'Redlands' quarry. Extensive sidings were laid between the branch and the road one mile east of Hook Norton station. Originally, two gas-fired drying kilns were erected on this site and later two more were added. A steam operated lift hoisted the loaded skips to the top of the kilns where a rotary tipper dumped the ore into the top for calcining. Chutes at the bottom allowed the dried ore to be loaded direct onto railway wagons.

When calcining was discontinued in 1926, the quarry tubs traversed around a gallery, and again by the use of a rotary tipper, emptied the raw ore into railway wagons marshalled underneath the gallery. The Ordnance Survey map reproduced as No. 13, gives the layout of both railway track and quarry working well.

Fig 39

Map 13

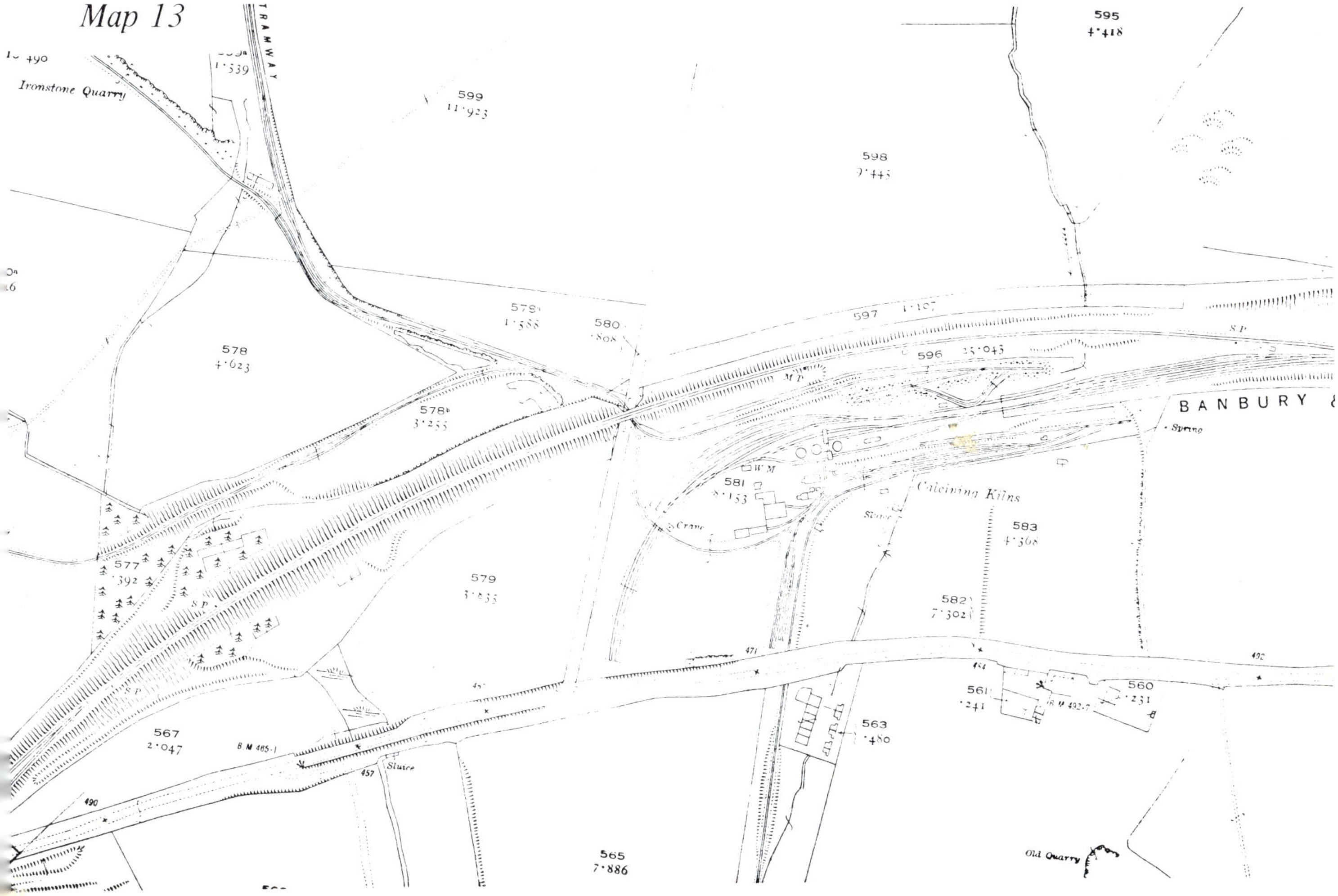

Four pictures reproduced here by courtesy of Messrs. Packer of Chipping Norton, give a good impression of the Brymbo quarry workings, and indeed are representative of the kilns erected both at Astrop and Sydenham Sidings. In **Figure 40** the 0-4-2 saddle tank *Joan* is shown at the quarry face with a long line of tubs. She is seen again in **Figure 41**, obviously posed for the photograph in the sunshine, just prior to running down to Brymbo sidings. Two of the heavy machines form the subject for **Figure 42**. On the right is the large steam navvy and, to the left and behind, is the big rotary stone crusher, which was used to reduce the size of the rock lumps as quarried and to separate the subsoil from the ore. At the bottom of the page is another picture of the four kilns, and the tub hoist and tippers can be seen mounted at the top of the retorts. After all these years, the names on the Private Owner wagons are of interest, including Robert Heath and Low Moor, Sheltons of Etruria, Margam Steel and Baldwins. Perhaps it is relevant to mention here that the trackage of the Brymbo quarries was all to 2′ gauge. The locomotive stud consisted of two Hudswell Clarke saddle tanks *Gwen* and *Joan,* an ex ROD 4-6-0 similar to the one at Sydenham, a tiny 0-4-0ST of Hunslet manufacture called *Betty* and a large 2-6-2 tank called *Russell* which came from the Welsh Highland Railway and is now preserved at Towyn in Merioneth.

One mile further along the line to the west from Brymbo Sidings, was Hook Norton itself. The station was built on a large embankment to get sufficient elevation to cross two deep valleys by means of viaducts, and to pierce the escarpment on the west side of the village by a 940 yard tunnel. Ironstone was also quarried here in two places, one at the east end of the station and opened in 1889 when the line was completed, the other to the south of the second viaduct and owned by the Earl of Dudley. The quarry at the east end was served by a standard gauge line which ran from the pits, under the high viaduct and up a severe incline to the station sidings. A six coupled tank engine called *Hook Norton* was purchased new from Manning Wardles, and was kept in a shed close by the station (see photo on **page 41**).

The ore in this area was soon exhausted and further pits were opened to the north-west of the station, where an extensive 1′ 8″ tramway was laid, passing under the road and running to a tipping dock alongside the standard gauge track underneath the viaduct. This early quarry with its complicated workings only survived until 1904 when the company failed and *Hook Norton* was absorbed into the GWR where she worked boat train traffic at Weymouth until 1926. The other pit at the south of the viaducts calcined its ore in a kiln under the second viaduct, which was then worked up to a railway siding by means of a rope incline with double tracks, full tubs up one track, empties down the other, motive power being a two-cylinder steam engine, supplied by two vertical boilers. A further double track incline was used for transporting coal down to this incline machinery. Work commenced in 1901 and closed down in 1916, and all the gear was dismantled by Friswells of Banbury in 1920.

Fig 40

Fig 41

Fig 43

Fig 42

Fig 44

Hook Norton

The photographs in the next four pages show Hook Norton station in the days of 1945-52. Figure 44 is to the east end of the station with the bridge carrying the railway over the road and in the distance can be seen Brymbo kilns. A good view of the signal box is in Figure 46 and the main station building on the Down side is depicted in Figure 47.

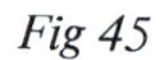

Fig 45

Fig 46

Fig 47

Map 14

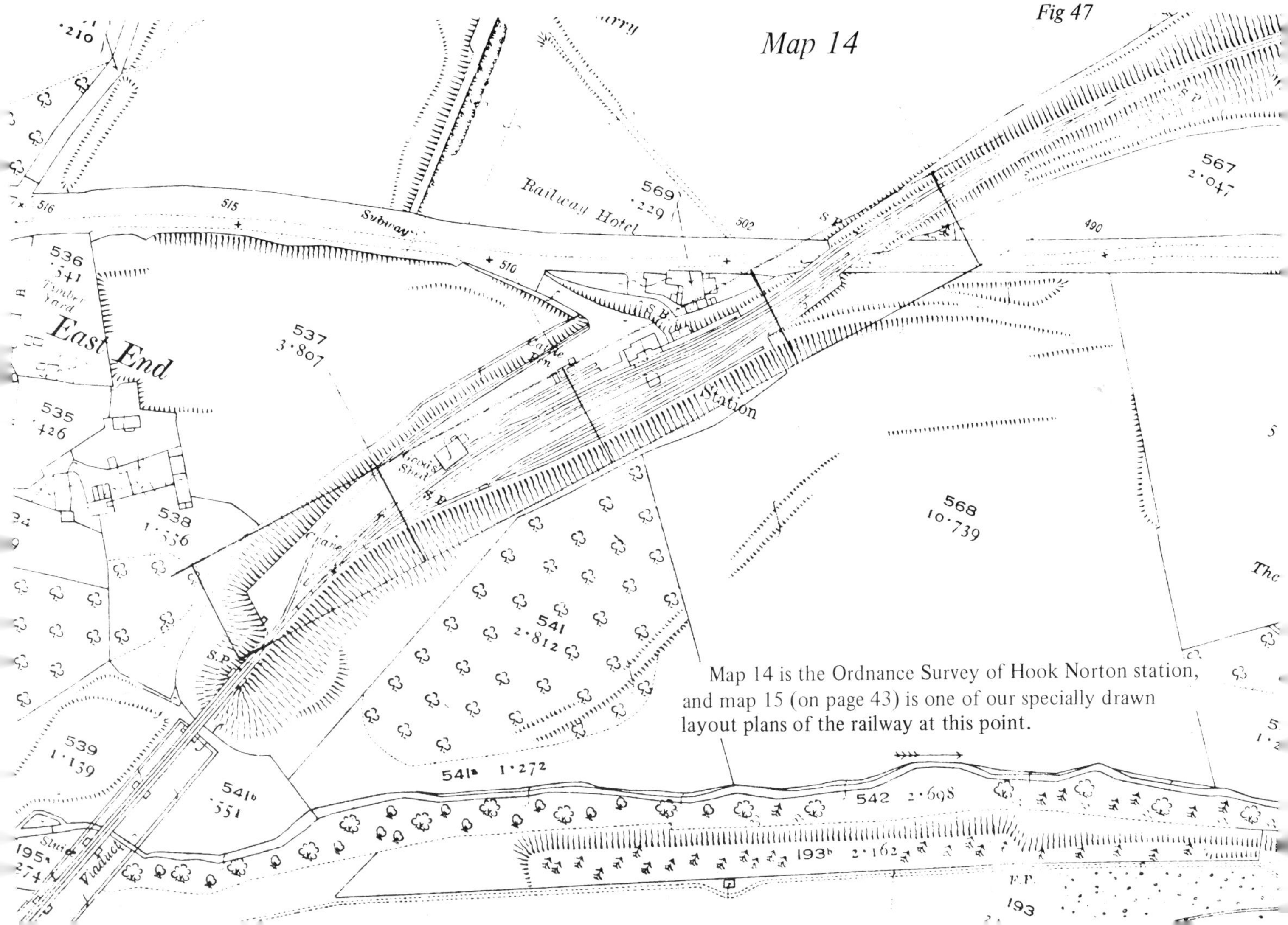

Map 14 is the Ordnance Survey of Hook Norton station, and map 15 (on page 43) is one of our specially drawn layout plans of the railway at this point.

A general view of the station, still facing east, is shown in Figure 48, whilst retreating further towards the viaducts, the cattle loading dock comes into sight on the left of Figure 49. Still further back, Figure 50 shows the 'Railway Inn' to the left of the station. Notice the sleeper foundation, bottom right, which was for railing the mobile platelayers trolley on to the track. The bottom photograph was taken from the top of the Home signal and gives a good impression of the yard layout. (Figure 51.)

Fig 48

Fig 49

Fig 50

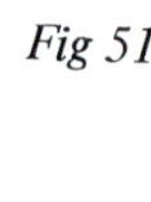

Fig 51

Fig 52

Fig 53

Page 39 consists of views all looking westwards, towards Rollright. Figure 52 is taken from the middle of the track looking between the platforms, whilst in Figure 53 more details are visible on the signal box. Standing on the cattle dock and looking towards the goods shed, the view is that of Figure 54. Note that the two sets of viaducts can just be seen beyond the signals and Figure 55 gives slightly more detail of the goods shed, with the mile post reading 91½ miles.

Fig 54

Fig 55

Fig 56

Fig 57

At the top of this page, the front (or rear) of the station can be seen as one approached up the station road. Figure 57 is of No. 1337 *Hook Norton* pictured at Weymouth after being absorbed into the Great Western Railway system. In Figure 58 the goods shed acts as a background to the single-line staff pick-up post and, for the uninitiated, the dog-kennel looking box (bottom right) was the storage place for the platelayers' tools. Finally, a close-up of the platform level signal box at Hook Norton, painted two shades of stone buff when I knew it. (Figure 59.)

Fig 58

Fig 59

An old G.W.R. Parcel label found at Hook Norton station.

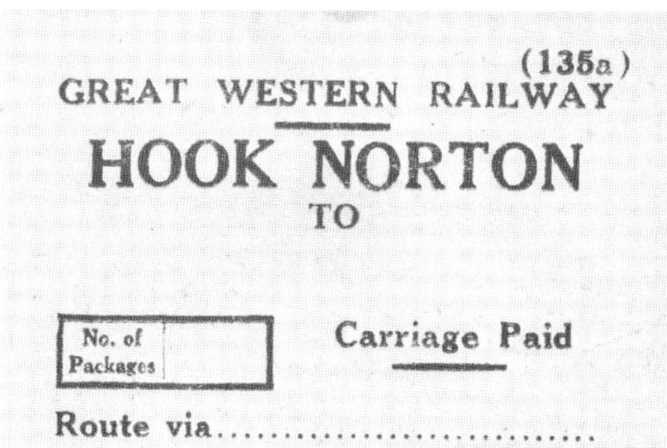

(135a)
GREAT WESTERN RAILWAY
HOOK NORTON
TO

No. of Packages

Carriage Paid

Route via.............................

Map 15

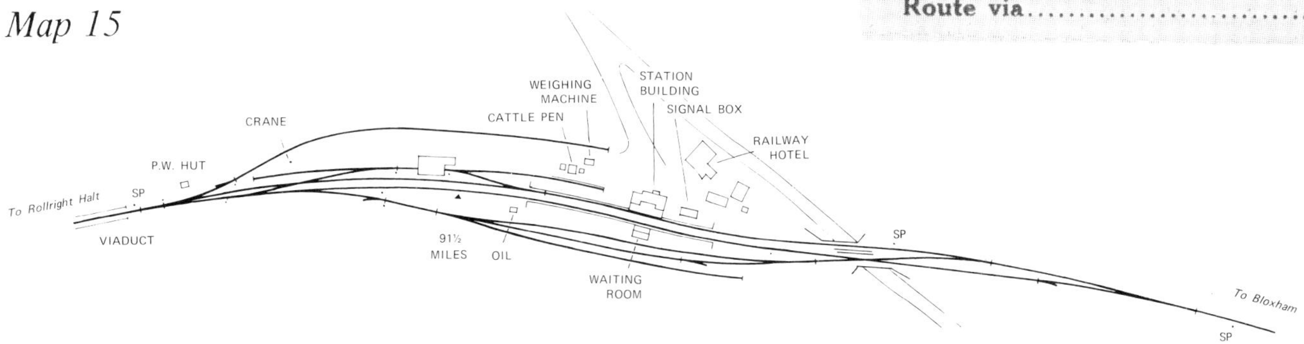

Hook Norton

Fig 60

Fig 61

Fig 62

The Viaducts, Hook Norton.

Fig 63

Fig 64

Fig 65

Having covered the Hook Norton station reasonably well, we now move on to those two slender, single track viaducts, both 90′ high, which spanned the valley between the station and tunnel. It is on record that these high structures took 400 men four years to construct, and, upon closure, four men with flame cutters four weeks to demolish, although the stone pillars still stand! One of the viaducts has eight spans and the other five. I have been able to cover them well pictorially, because, wishing to model this section of the line in 1947, I gathered together many photographs taken from all angles, enabling a reasonable miniature to be constructed. Figure 61, however, is a very early photograph which not only shows a train of five 4-wheel carriages crossing over, but also the single kiln and ropeway mentioned before, connected with the Earl of Dudley's iron ore workings. The other two pictures show both sides of the viaduct nearest Hook Norton station, and in Figures 64 and 65 we show the entrance and exit of Hook Norton tunnel.

This page is concerned exclusively with details of the construction of the high girders, and Figure 66 shows the first span, with Hook Norton church framed in the arch. Figure 67 is of the entrance to the viaduct and one should note the longitudinal sleepers and derailment guard rails on each side of the running rail.

Fig 66

Fig 67

Fig 68

Fig 69

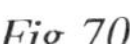

Fig 70

The girderwork in close detail can be seen in Figure 68, and in Figure 69 the abutment and end pillars are shown. Finally, in the lower left picture, it is possible to notice the catwalk which was used by the permanent way ganger on his daily inspection of the ironwork. (Figure 70.)

Before leaving these bridges, it may be of interest to recall the method of testing the viaducts for load deflection. This was by coupling four 2-8-0 class engines together and running them at speed over the whole length of track, from tunnel to station, an alarming experience for both onlooker and enginemen alike!

Rollright Halt

After passing through Hook Norton tunnel, the branch wanders across the valley of the Swer, gradually climbing, until it reaches a height of 600 feet, a short level stretch, and then the line starts to fall until reaching Rollright Halt. This little layout was in two parts. Moving westward, one came to the goods sidings, which consisted of a single track alongside the branch line. Access to the siding was by means of a ground frame, opened by inserting a key on the end of the single-line staff into the keyway on the frame, releasing the levers for moving the points. Rollright Siding was equipped with two loading gauges, a loading ramp, a goods shed, and a weighbridge, all of which can be seen in the pictures on this page. (Figures 71 to 74.)

Fig 71

Fig 72

Fig 73

Fig 74

Map 16

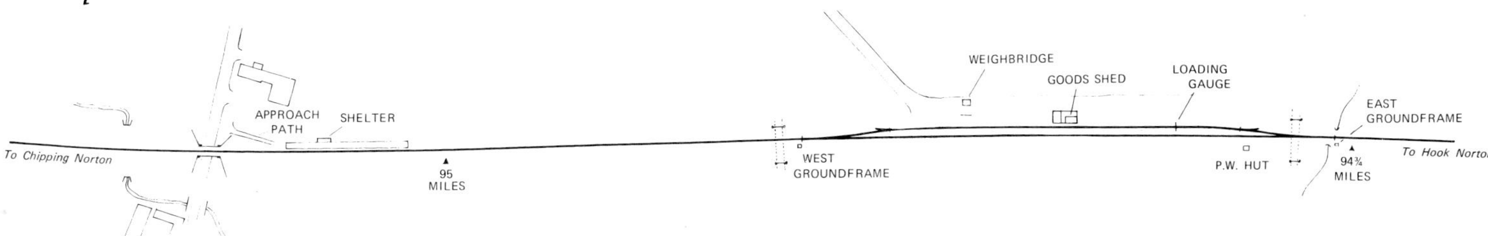

Rollright Halt

Fig 75

Fig 76

No.16 sketch map gives the layout of this tiny outpost of the GWR system and Figure 76 shows one of the two ground frames which let traffic in and out of the siding. A quarter of a mile further west was the wooden platform and iron 'Pagoda' style shelter of Rollright Halt. Figure 75 shows it in all its stark simplicity. Leaving Rollright, the branch still descended at an average 1 in 80 gradient until reaching Chipping Norton tunnel. It was a frightfully wet bore with water cascading from the roof in many places, not a very pleasant duty having to apply the hand brake at the open end of a goods brake van, at the rear of a descending ore train, especially with the combination of engine fumes, brake dust and dirty water. After 750 yards of this, the line suddenly emerges from the blackness, straight into the platforms of Chipping Norton station.

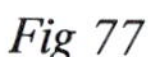

Fig 77

Fig 78

Fig 79

Chipping Norton

Among the many pictures that I was lucky enough to take on the 'Kingham' branch were the three illustrated here. I had just finished getting a nice shot of the east end of the Chipping Norton tunnel in Figure 78, when I heard a train approaching. On turning completelyround amongst the waist-high rose-bay willow-herb, I managed to secure the picture in Figure 77 of No. 7335 against the bright sunshine trundling the five wagons and a van into the tunnel behind me. This was the daily local 'pick-up' goods.

The lower photograph is the view the engineman would have after negotiating this tunnel and breaking out into the daylight, with Chipping Norton station itself. (Figure 79.)

Map 17

Map 17 is the Ordnance Survey of Chipping Norton station about the year 1899, showing the adjacent land, and tweed mills.

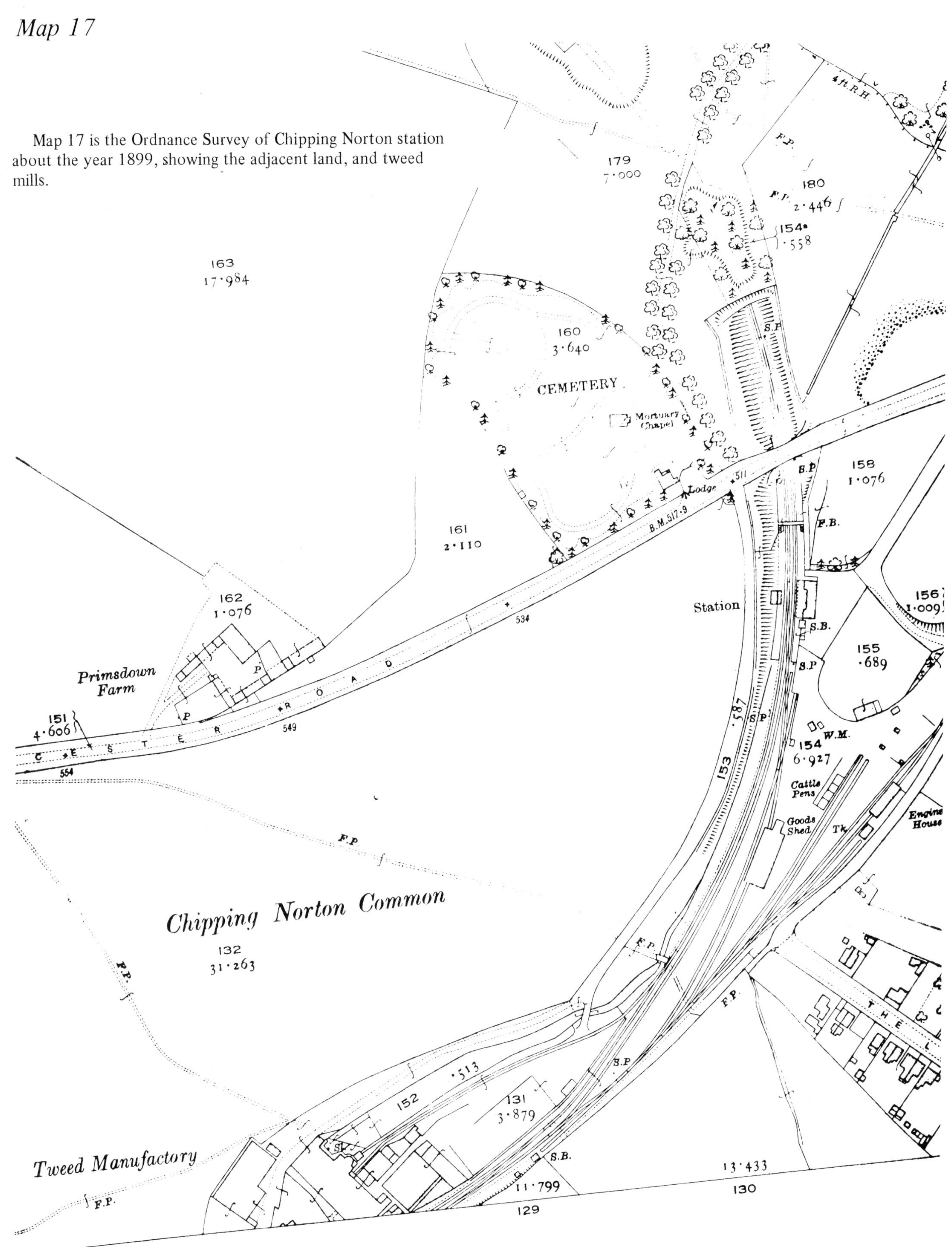

Map 18 on this page is our own prepared track layout sketch, and again the date would be at the turn of the century.

Map 18

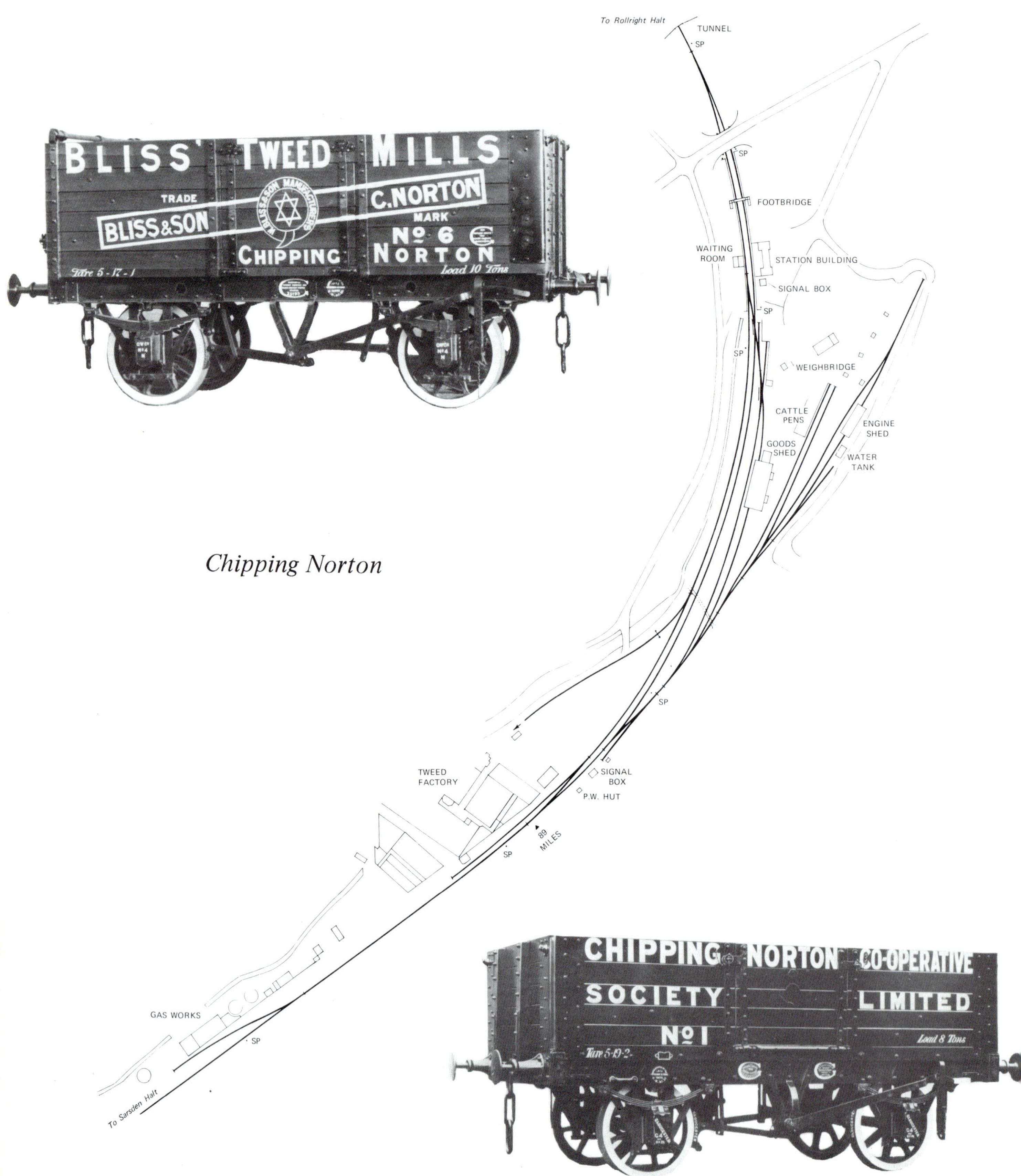

Chipping Norton

Fig 80

Fig 81

Following the practice of walking backwards in imagination, Figure 80 gives a good impression of the south portal of the tunnel with the Home signal and facing points in the immediate foreground. This is the view from the Chipping Norton—Moreton-in-Marsh road bridge at the north end of the station. Retreating towards Kingham, this bridge comes into the picture in Figure 81 and one can also see the Down-side water tower on the left, and the Starting signal on the right, with its attendant 'shunt' arm. A little further south along the Up platform the lattice girder bridge comes into the picture. Note the two gas lamps at each end, mounted on short ornamental bases and sitting directly on the top of the lattice work. (Figure 82.) Crossing to the Down platform, and still looking north, the main station building and signal box are shown in Figure 83. Incidentally, in the period I knew it, 1930-50, all the paintwork was of standard two tone GWR stone buff, masonry was red brick with blue bases, and roofs of slate.

Fig 82

Fig 83

Fig 84

Looking across the tracks, Figure 84 shows the Down platform, waiting room, gardens and seat. The track fittings in between the platform faces is that of the top crossover, which, by virtue of a single compound point, led also to the goods shed and yard. Figure 85 was taken even further along the track and indicates where this pointwork branched off to both goods shed and long siding. From the latter it was possible to gain access to the loading dock seen at top right.

Fig 85

Climbing to the top of the Up starting signal produced the scene in Figure 86. It shows the large red brick goods shed and the water-cum-coaling stage on the far right. Still further towards Kingham, the approach to all the yard sidings can be seen, with the running lines on the left and the siding entering Bliss's Tweed Mills. (Figure 87.)

Fig 86

Fig 87

Fig 88

Fig 89

Fig 90

The final shot taken from the tall Down Home signal, gives a good picture of the yard layout. The facing point in the foreground is the lead to the goods yard and the division of Up and Down running lines can be seen just in front of the pedestrian crossing. (Figure 88.)

The photograph alongside (Figure 89) is a companion high level picture and the two together do give a clear viewpoint of the track layout at Chipping Norton. Figure 90 is a close-up detail of the right-of-way pedestrian crossing which had to be maintained by the railway company because, on building the line, the tracks cut across an established footpath. (This can be traced on map No. 17.)

A page of contrast, but all dealing with Chipping Norton station. Figures 91-93 show three views of the area taken in the 1910-12 period. In those days, there were two signal boxes, one on the platform and another smaller version at the western end of the station limits. (See Figure 100.) Also, the distant signal arms at that time were painted red with a white stripe, not the yellow and black, which came later.

Fig 91

Fig 92

Fig 93

Figure 93 is of great interest because not only does it show a private owner wagon in the siding at Bliss's (bottom right) but also one can just see the early '517' class shunting in the yard, and the small train of two maroon painted 4-wheel carriages standing on the running line.

Figure 94 is included because it shows the unusual water tank, the bottom half of which was a coaling stage and the site of the locomotive shed which used to exist where the corrugated iron sheets are seen in the photograph. I was told that this small shed was a single line 'through' type, capable of holding two small tank engines and was built in yellow brick with blue brick base.

Fig 94

Fig 95

Fig 96

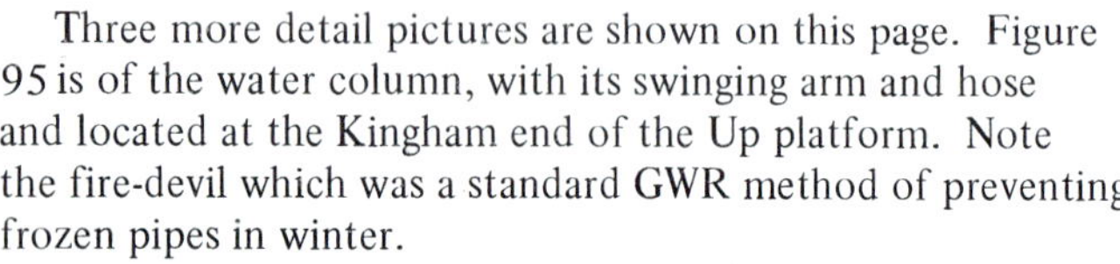

Three more detail pictures are shown on this page. Figure 95 is of the water column, with its swinging arm and hose and located at the Kingham end of the Up platform. Note the fire-devil which was a standard GWR method of preventing frozen pipes in winter.

Pick-up and set-down arms for the single-line staff are seen in Figure 96, not those at Chipping Norton, these were the Bloxham equipment! The station facade is shown, as seen from the approach road, in Figure 97. Modellers should note, however, that a canopy used to extend from gutter level out over the doorway, and the building had two centre windows.

Fig 97

Through the courtesy of Messrs. Packers of Chipping Norton, who have been taking photographs in that town for almost a century, I enclose two staff pictures of quite unusual character. The large picture in Figure 98 is of a certain Sgt. Baker (in uniform) on the occasion of a recruiting drive in the First World War period. The caption states there were three volunteers, but I can only leave the reader to guess who they were! Obviously the train crew are those stationed on the engine's running plate, and among the group of four on the right, surely two would belong to the platelaying gang. But of the others, who can say? If any reader recognises a friend or relative, I would like to know.

Fig 98

Fig 99

The other unusual photograph in Figure 99 is of No. 1473 *Fair Rosamund*, complete with enginemen and station staff, standing in the Down platform at Chipping Norton. But, why was it away from the Woodstock Branch? Could it be a special excursion from Oxford, or even Blenheim? I'm sure she did not work regularly over the Kingham line, as she was always rostered for the Oxford-Kidlington-Woodstock branch. (Note the chocolate and cream six-wheeled composite carriage, with central luggage compartment behind the engine.)

Figure 100 is captioned 'The derailment at Chipping Norton', interesting in that it is the only picture located of Chipping Norton West Box. If one refers to the Survey map on page 49, it will be seen that there was a short dead end siding here and I would assume that the engine and van were intended for the running line, but were over eager, and wrongly thinking that the road was set for them, steamed off and ran out of track! For the interested, the engine is No. 546 and the goods brake van is branded 'Wolverhampton'.

Fig 100

Fig 101

The top picture is rather nice, showing both 'The Leys' just after the houses had been built in that lane going straight up from the railway, and some 'Private Owner' wagons being shunted in the yard. Note the Chipping Norton Co-op Society's coal wagon No. 1 at the left. I would date this photograph in the 1930s. The two lower photographs were taken in 1947 and show No. 5361 on the local goods train and No. 6137 on the Chipping Norton-Kingham local passenger run.

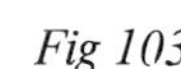

Fig 103

Fig 102

Sarsden Halt

Fig 104

Leaving Chipping Norton, the line headed south-westwards again on a slightly falling gradient, following the course of the Sarsden brook closely, and after approximately two miles came to Sarsden Halt. This small timber-platformed calling place, with iron pagoda, was installed to serve the village of Churchill just to the south-east of the line. Logically it should have been named 'Churchill Halt' but the landowner, Earl Ducie, who lived at Sarsden House beyond Churchill, requested that the little halt be 'Sarsden Halt' and so it was. (Map 19.)

The pictures on this page are looking slightly towards Chipping Norton from the south-east and it is possible to see the complete layout together with the signal box, which sat at the Kingham end of the platform. This box, when I knew it, was not a block post in the true sense of the word. Its levers operated the points to the yard, but only by insertion of the train staff, similar to a ground frame. Nevertheless, it did have two distant signals to operate, which were worked in conjunction with the crossing gates. So to sum up, the railwayman in charge at Sarsden Halt, was in reality a crossing keeper-cum-porter, who could let traffic in and out of the goods siding, but only by use of the staff.

Map 19

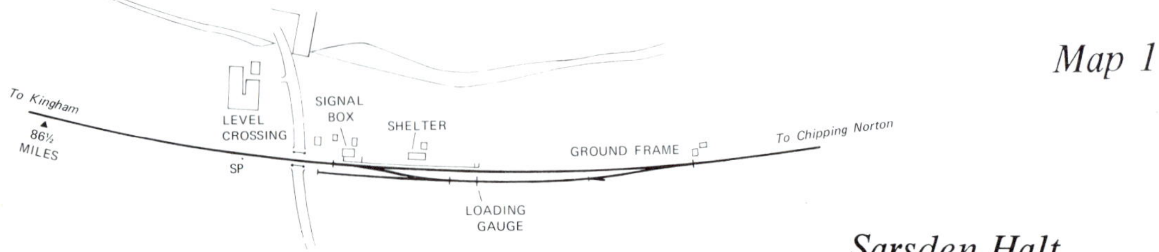

Sarsden Halt

Fig 105

Fig 106

Fig 107

Fig 108

Fig 109

Fig 110

This might be a good place to mention that, on a single line like the Banbury-Cheltenham, all distant signals were fixed and could not be lowered to 'Clear'. The exceptions were those controlling level crossings, which were lowered when the gates were closed to road traffic. Figure 109 shows one of these latter signals protecting 'Churchill Crossing', where the road from Churchill to Kingham crossed the branch.

The lower photograph is of Sarsden Halt in the last days and shows 2-6-2T working the local service (Figure 110.)

Fig 111

Kingham

Two miles further to the south-west, and Kingham station was reached or rather the junction and signal box known as 'Kingham East'. In Figure 111 we see the junction, with the double lines going off to the right, over the flyover bridge to avoid the station, and so on towards Cheltenham. Just before reaching Kingham East box, the single line became double and then divided again as can be seen, the Up and Down lines bearing off left to enter Kingham station. In the late 1950s, the avoiding line was reduced to single track and is shown in this condition in Figure 112.

Fig 112

Fig 113

Figure 113 shows a 517 class 0-4-2T No. 835 at Kingham on the "Chippy branch" train. In Figure 114 the Chipping Norton platforms at Kingham are seen, although it should be pointed out that this is in BR days. As I knew it, a double junction was installed at the end of the platform to give access to both main line and Cheltenham branch.

As recorded in the historical section, Kingham station was originally named 'Chipping Norton Junction' and only changed to Kingham around the First World War period, owing to confusion caused to passengers by the two similar names.

Fig 114

Map 20

The early Survey map No. 20 is dated approximately 1870, and it will be seen that much to and fro shunting had to take place before a train from Chipping Norton could proceed on to the Bourton-on-the-Water branch. Note also that at this time no engine shed was shown.

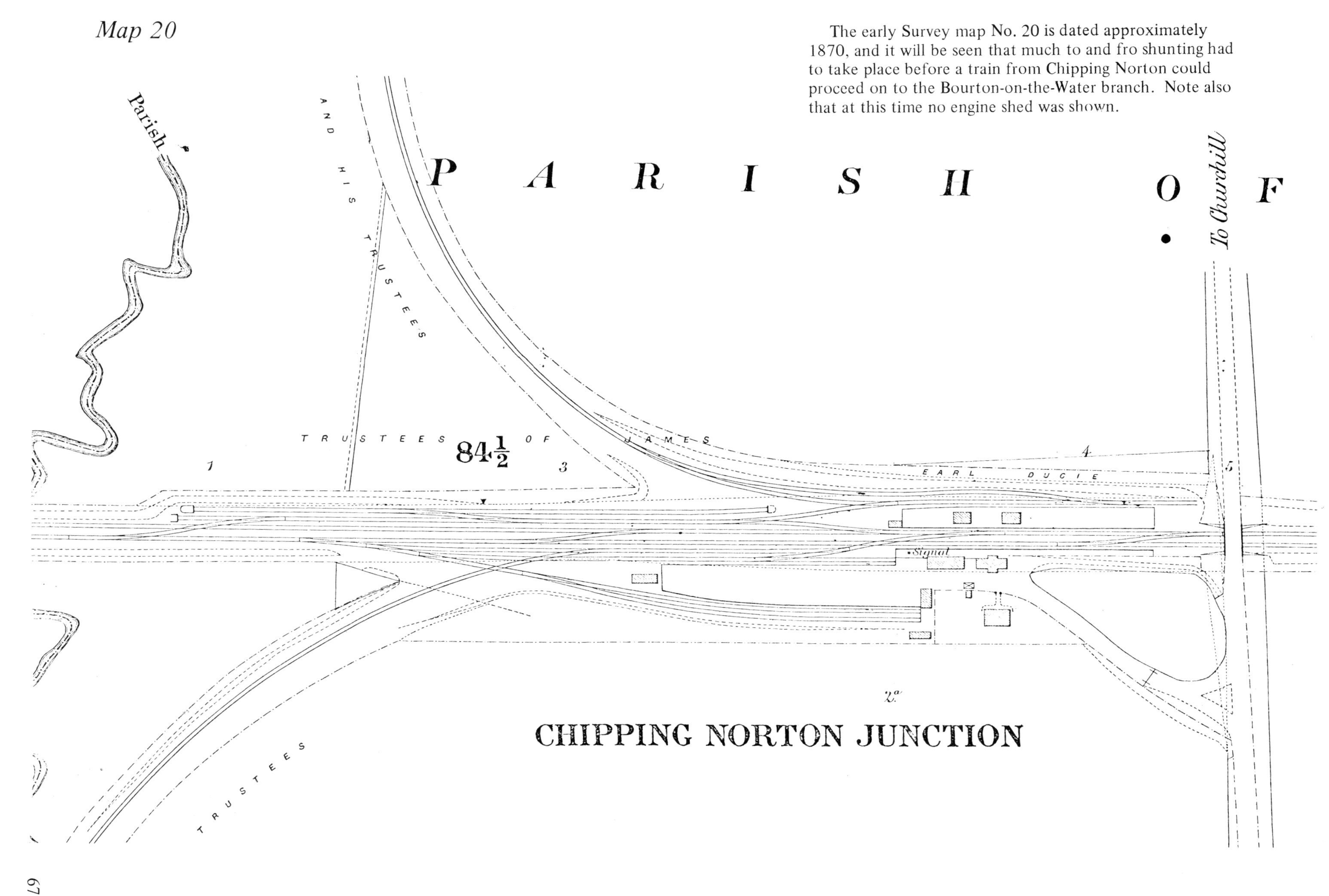

Map 21

The second Survey map No. 21 is dated approximately 1920 and shows the layout at its fullest development (without the 1939-45 wartime sidings, of course). Note now, the double avoiding line at the top, the loco shed, and turntable, in fact double lines everywhere plus cattle pens and sidings at the Oxford end.

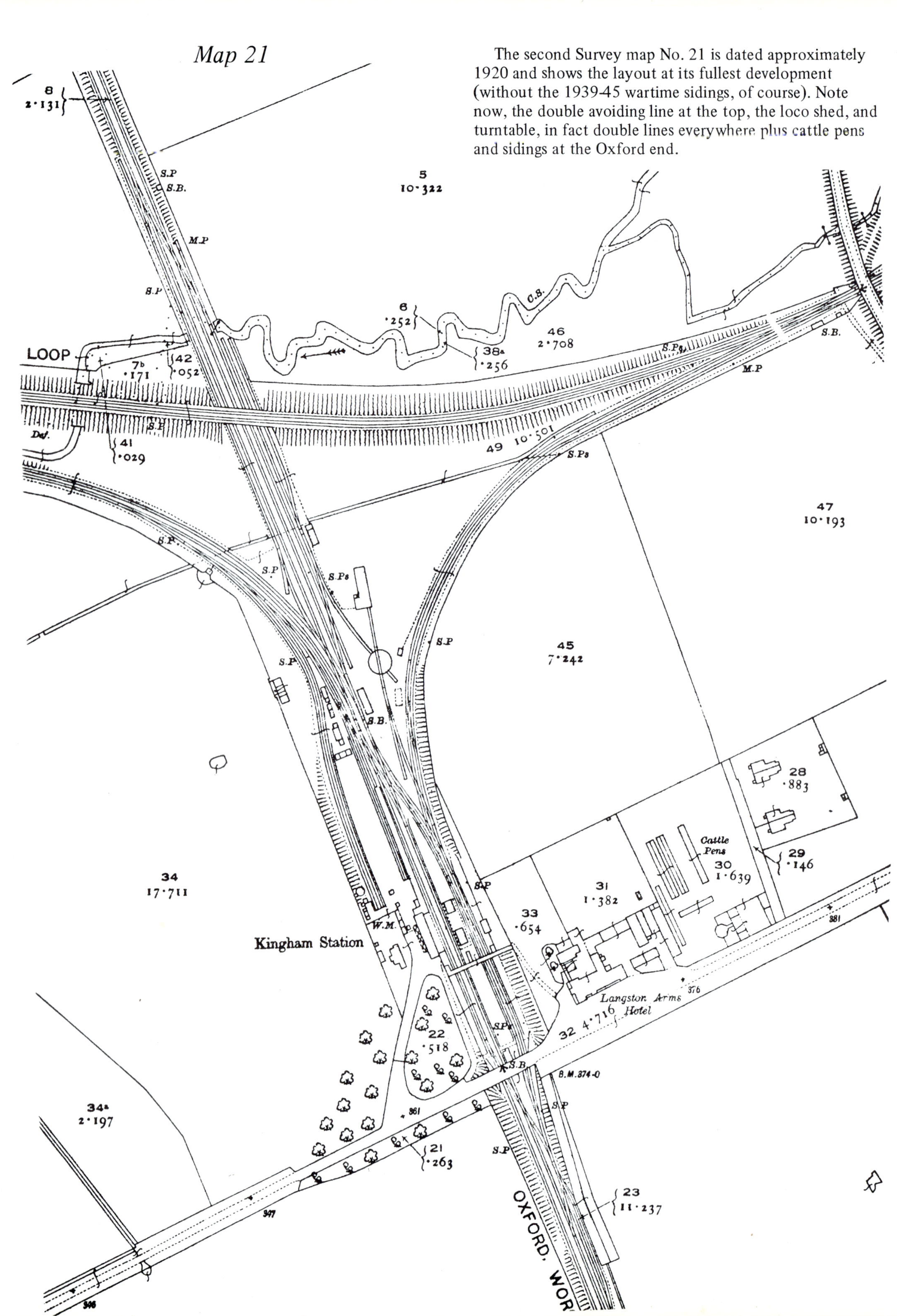

Fig 115

Fig 116

Two early photographs of Chipping Norton Junction are shown in Figures 115 and 116, the top picture looking south and the centre picture looking towards the north. I would date both these views at 1908 each with several points of interest. There was a signal box on the island platform, towering above the road bridge against which it was built, at the south end of the station. It can just be seen behind the main starting signal in the top picture. Note the three-arm bracket signals which abounded and the station lighting by oil lamps. By contrast, Figure 117 shows 'Kingham' station in the 1950s with electricity installed, name-board altered, and signals with indicator panels in place of separate arms.

Fig 117

Another picture taken in BR days is that in Figure 118. This is still looking south down the main line towards Oxford. On the left is the two-coach train for Chipping Norton headed by 2-6-2 tank No. 4141, whilst standing on the Down main is a '61XX' class tank engine, with one Brake 3rd carriage! Gone were the days when the Worcester express slipped a rake of main line stock at Kingham to be rushed post haste over the Bourton branch and MSW joint line to the Spa.

Figure 119 is of the signal box, loco shed, water tower and junction area, looking north towards Worcester. The Chipping Norton branch goes off to the right and the Cheltenham line to the left, date 1956.

Fig 118

Fig 119

Looking in the same direction from the height of the footbridge, in the 1920s, Figure 120 also shows the mixture of slate and lead used on the station roofs.

The facade of Kingham Junction is seen in Figure 121 but again in British Railways days. Note the two-colour brickwork of yellow and blue tone, rather unusual for the Great Western Railway.

Fig 120
Fig 121

Fig 122

Fig 123

In Figure 122, No. 78009, one of the British Railways class 2 locomotives, is shown outside the small engine shed at Kingham. This shed, not erected until 1913, was a small affair with one track capable of holding two locomotives. Originally a turntable was installed in the approach road, but this was removed just after the Second World War.

Figure 123 gives a good impression of the actual siting of the shed and water tower, in the small triangle formed by the apex of the main, avoiding and Chipping Norton lines.

Taken from behind the signal box, the large water tower shows up well in this detail shot. It was of necessity massive, for not only did it supply a water column outside the shed, but also one at each end of the platforms. The painting of this tank was the usual light and dark stone colour in the period I knew it, 1930-50, but in BR days this was changed to a pale daffodil colour with black lower parts. (Figure 124.)

Fig 124

Fig 125

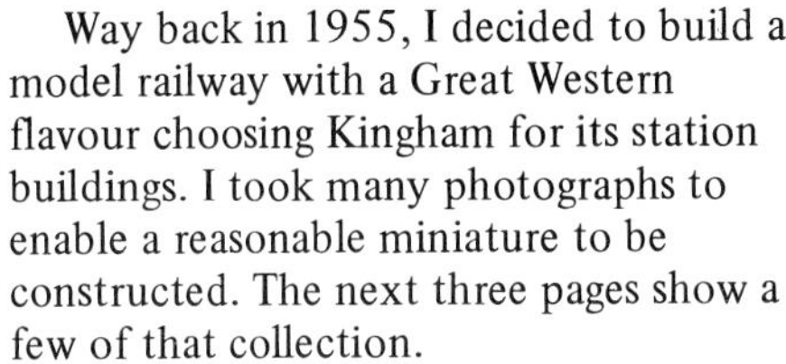

Way back in 1955, I decided to build a model railway with a Great Western flavour choosing Kingham for its station buildings. I took many photographs to enable a reasonable miniature to be constructed. The next three pages show a few of that collection.

Figure 125 looks down at the main station building from the footbridge, with the parcels office at extreme left and next door the various staff rooms. In Figure 126 we see the booking office on the left which was combined with the waiting room and alongside this, the ladies room. Extreme right was the station master's large office followed by the gentlemen's lavatory. (Figure 127.) The station awning was made quite light and airy by having glass panels in the roof and these are shown to advantage in Figure 128.

Fig 126

Fig 128

Fig 127

Fig 129

Fig 130

Fig 131

A second look at the parcels office and waiting room is taken in Figure 129 and it can be noticed that the small blue brick platform blocks have now been changed for the 2′ square concrete slabs. Figure 130 is of the facade again, but looking back at it from the north. In the next illustration we have a close-up of the aforementioned Gents, with the porters quarters next door (Figure 131.)

Having covered the main building quite well, now a few pictures dealing with the island structure. In Figure 132 we again look towards Oxford. The first small room was a storage place which backed on to the 'Ladies' waiting room.

Fig 132

Fig 133

The other end of the building, seen in Figure 133, was of course the gentlemen's lavatory which backed onto the general waiting room. Figure 134 shows that the whole affair consisted of two brick built structures with a girder roof, stretching over and between them, with a circulating area in the centre. The lower illustrations give some idea of the girder and roofwork on these buildings.

Fig 134

Fig 135

Fig 136

Figure 137 is of interest in this series of Kingham, for it shows the actual siting of the old Kingham South signal box. Those few white marks on the bridge abutment between the two starting signals, are all that is left of one of the tall early cabins which controlled the Oxford end of the station. The train on the left has just arrived from Cheltenham.

The unusual bracket signal in Figure 138 is that which used to be located at the Worcester end of the Down platform, constructed in this fashion to enable enginemen to get a good sighting under that road bridge seen in the top photograph.

Fig 137

Fig 138

Fig 139

Fig 140

Fig 141

A spread shot in Figure 139 perhaps gives its siting to better advantage, and in Figure 141 No. 5538 is shown standing at this same signal, before setting off along the Cheltenham branch to Stow.

The odd picture of the long line of Austerity 2-8-0 engines really does belong to this small book, because, directly after the Second World War, two of the lengthy sidings to the north of the avoiding line bridge at Kingham were used as stabling ground for these brand new engines, before their eventual disposal was decided upon. (Figure 140.)

Two important items of the single line working are illustrated on this page. Figure 142 on the left, is an example of the net variety of staff-catcher. The other type was in the form of a leather padded shape, but each had in common the protruding horn, upon which the enginemen had to set the incoming train-staff. In Figure 143 is the most important piece of equipment for single line working, the staff instrument. The signalman is seen in the act of withdrawing a staff, which he could only do with the co-operation of the next signal box.

Fig 142

Fig 143

Fig 144

Finally, in this photograph, we see the two-coach 'B' set, lined up awaiting the road to Cheltenham. For those interested, these two, branded 'Kingham Branch', were to Diagram E.140, Brake Composites, numbered 6894 and 6895. (Figure 144.)

Map 22

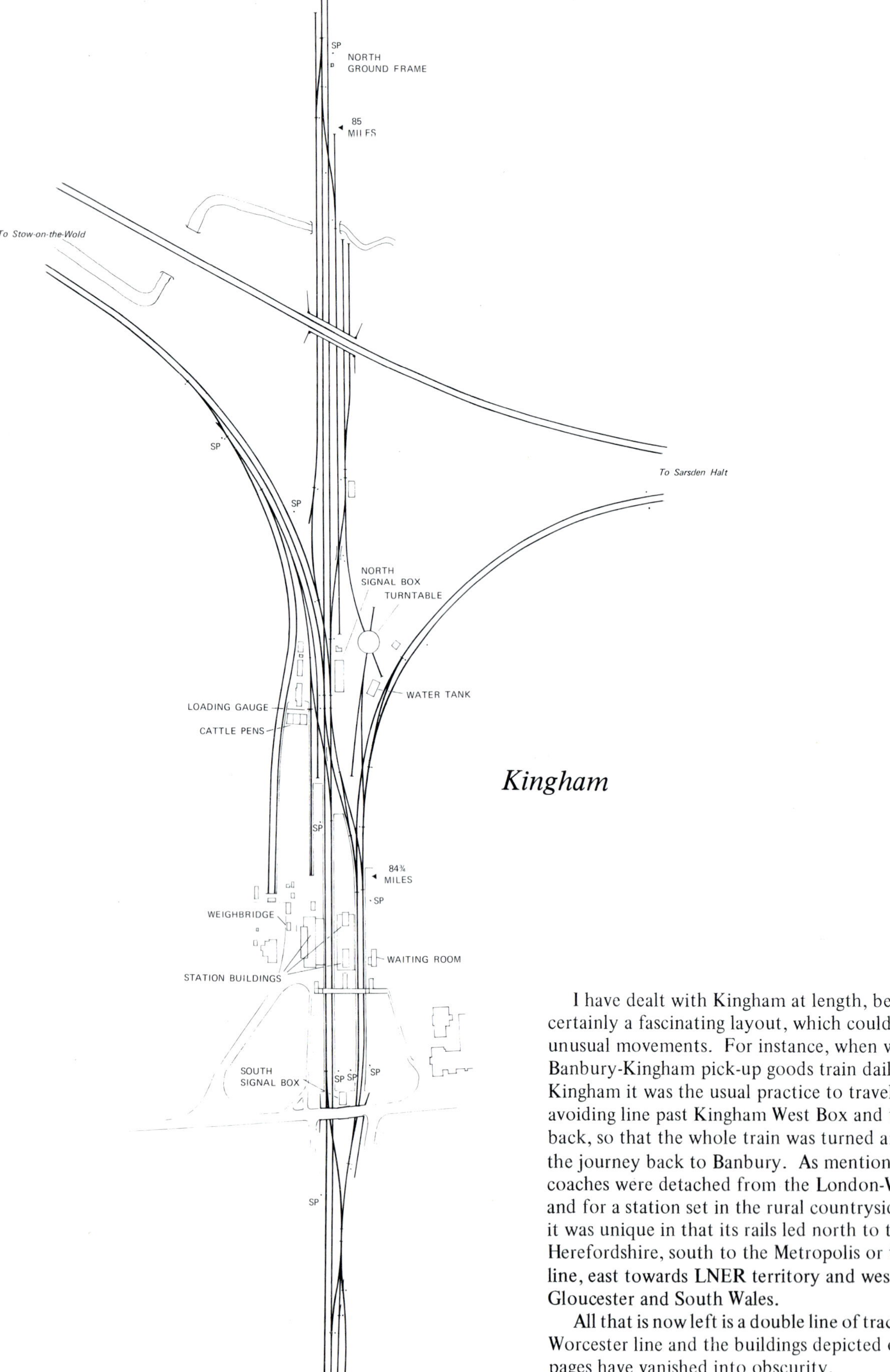

Kingham

I have dealt with Kingham at length, because it was certainly a fascinating layout, which could allow many unusual movements. For instance, when working the local Banbury-Kingham pick-up goods train daily, on arrival at Kingham it was the usual practice to travel first over the avoiding line past Kingham West Box and then reversing back, so that the whole train was turned around ready for the journey back to Banbury. As mentioned before, slip coaches were detached from the London-Worcester trains and for a station set in the rural countryside of Oxfordshire it was unique in that its rails led north to the Midlands and Herefordshire, south to the Metropolis or the Channel coast line, east towards LNER territory and west towards Gloucester and South Wales.

All that is now left is a double line of track on the Oxford-Worcester line and the buildings depicted on the previous pages have vanished into obscurity.

Map 22 is our prepared track layout of Kingham for 1915 onwards.

Figure 145 is the official photograph of Kingham engine shed and turntable. The avoiding line bridge can be seen in middle left.

G.W.R. KINGHAM WEST SIGNAL BOX.

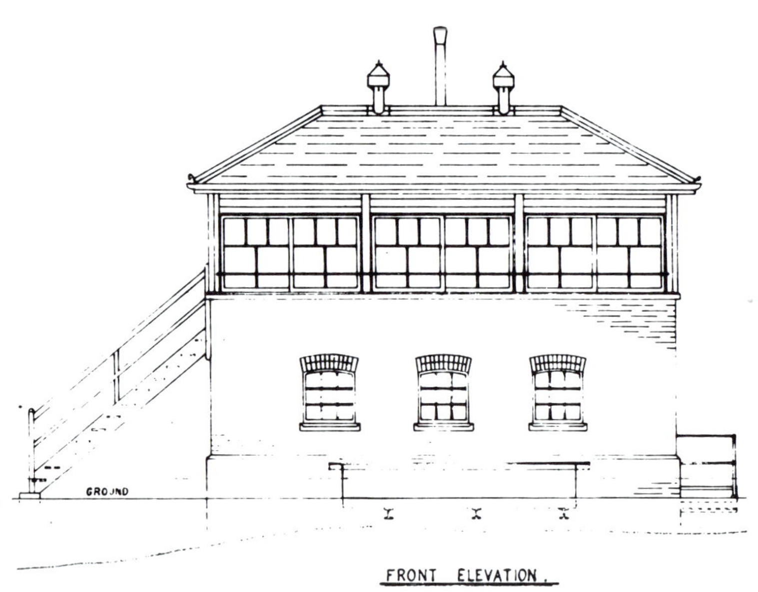

FRONT ELEVATION.

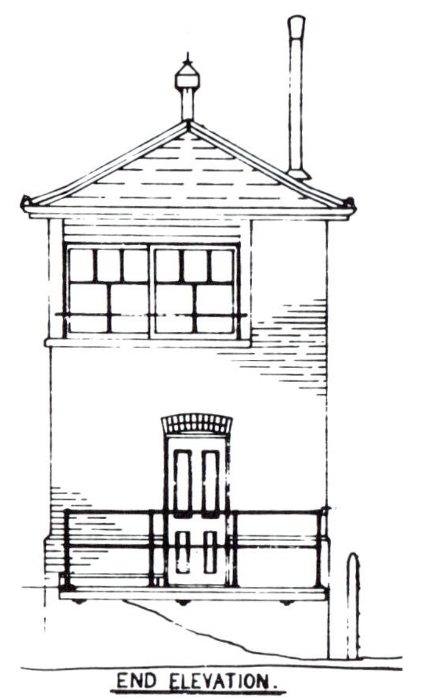
END ELEVATION.

Official British Rail drawing

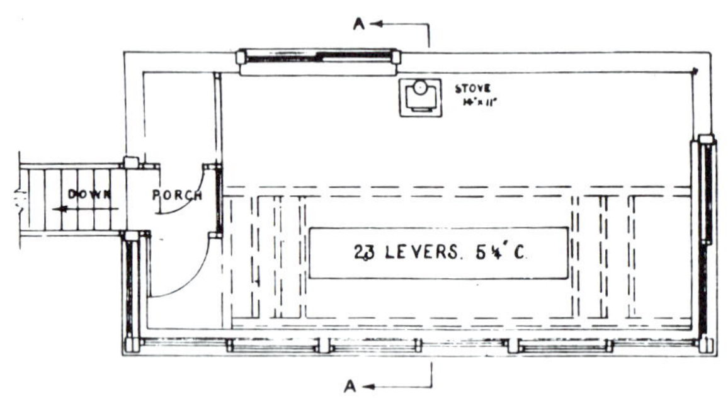

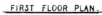

FIRST FLOOR PLAN.

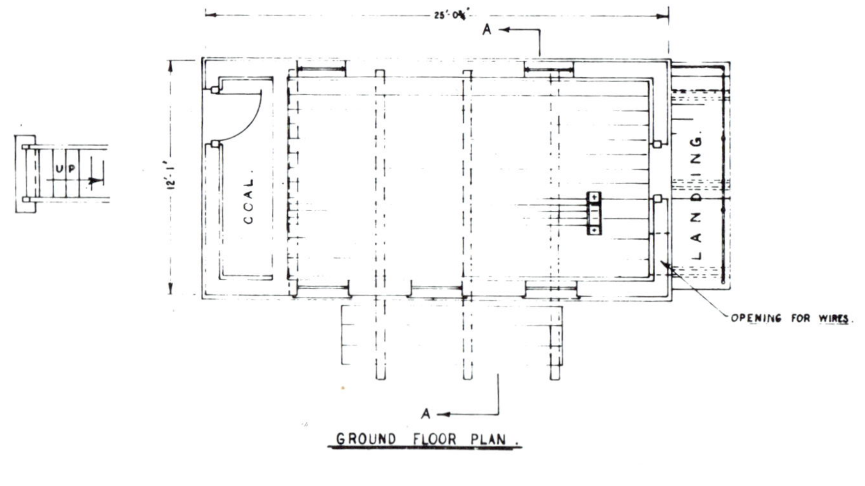

GROUND FLOOR PLAN.

DOWN

However, to continue our imaginary journey, leaving Kingham by the west curve on a double line track, the route runs to Kingham West signal box, where the avoiding line joins in. The branch once again becomes a single track as we head for Stow-on-the-Wold.

Fig 146

Stow-on-the-Wold

This small station is approached on a rising gradient and was actually on the 475′ contour line. The actual town of Stow was one mile to the north of the station at the top of a hill 765 feet above sea level and situated on the old Roman Fosse Way, which the railway follows from Stow to Bourton. (Map 23.)

Fig 147

The main station buildings of Stow and Bourton stations were rebuilt in the early 1930s and Stow can be seen in Figures 146 and 147. Very nicely executed in faced Cotswold stone, this building has since become a charming private residence!

Figure 148 shows the arrival of the Kingham-Cheltenham local train. The signal box, like Sarsden, was only a glorified ground frame and the large canopy alongside extended from the corrugated iron goods shed which is just visible behind.

Fig 148

Map 23

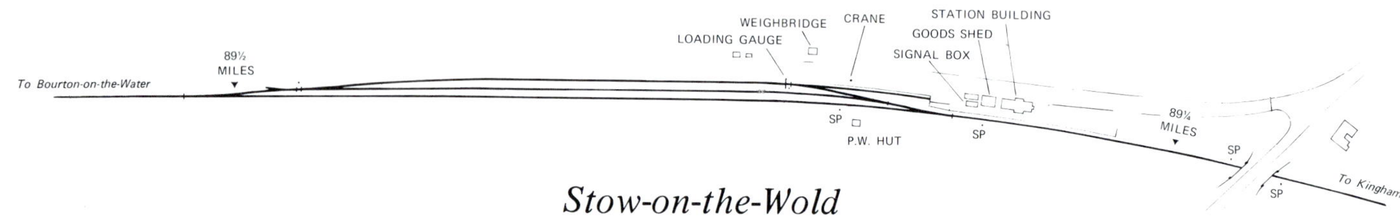

Stow-on-the-Wold

Fig 149

Fig 150

A close-up of the hand crane at Stow with its wooden jib can be studied in Figure 150.

The lower picture is also of Stow, but looking westward towards Bourton and one can notice the two sidings and loading dock, with the fixed hand crane thereon. (Figure 151.)

Fig 151

Fig 152

Fig 153

Two miles of downgrade and the line reaches Bourton-on-the-Water, situated on the lovely River Windrush. This was the terminus of the branch when first opened in 1862 and Figure 152 is an official photograph of the original half-timbered station building. This was taken prior to the construction of the new Cotswold stone erection seen in Figure 153. One can see at once the similarity between this and Stow.

Fig 154

This official picture of the platform side of the early Bourton station is included, although of poor quality, for the sake of comparison, as it ties up with the other two studies of the new building shown, Figures 155 and 156.

Bourton-on-the-Water

Fig 155

Fig 156

The final picture of the end section of the half-timbered station is seen in Figure 157. I particularly go for the Austin Seven parked outside, the property of the Station Master!

Fig 157

Fig 158

Figure 158 shows the view from the platform looking east, just prior to the replacement of the original station building. The lower view shows Bourton again but this time looking west some thirty years later.

Fig 159

Seen from the road bridge, the track layout is shown well from this high viewpoint. Notice the lattice post for the Down starting signal, Figure 160. Also Figure 161, from up on high, a view of the station approach and coal yard, with the weighbridge on the extreme right. Coming right down to track level, Figure 162 shows both platform faces, and No. 8491 with the local goods from Kingham, standing on the Down running line.

Fig 160

Fig 161

Fig 162

Fig 164

The pavilion-like shelter on the Up platform is seen from both angles in Figures 163 and 165. It was of timber construction and was in place even when the early station building was still standing. Figure 164 shows the water tank at Bourton, with its swing-arm column fixed underneath. This was the only water supply at this station, there being no columns on the platforms. The signal box, which was on the same side of the track as the water tank, was a typical GWR building of red brick, with blue brick footings and facings, and with wooden window frames and slated roof. (Figure 166.)

Fig 163

Fig 165

Fig 166

Fig 167

The goods shed at Bourton-on-the-Water was a large black timber building, set on brick plinths. As can be seen by the three pictures on this page, the building consisted of one high central shed with a single line of track running through on one side, whilst at the opposite side a loading bay was arranged, with an overhanging canopy (see Figure 164). At each end of the main structure were two smaller offices, one for the staff, and the other for valuable goods which had to be under lock and key. Figure 168 shows the end nearest Stow and the large swing doors, which closed off the shed track. As a bonus, there is a close-up of the single-line staff pick-up post in the foreground. The lamp with bull's-eye was to direct a beam of light on to the staff, to help the engine crew get an accurate fix for a pick-up. It might also be mentioned that the socket was hinged in the line of travel, to alleviate the sudden impact on a fireman's arm!

Fig 168

Fig 169

Map 24 gives the track layout at Bourton-on-the-Water. As a bonus, the signal box frame plan is reproduced on this page.

Map 24

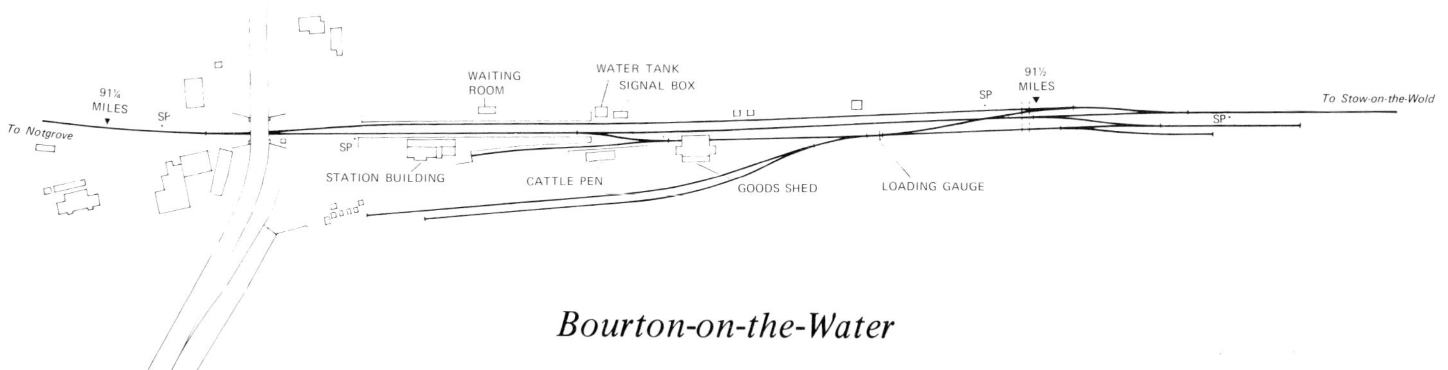

Bourton-on-the-Water

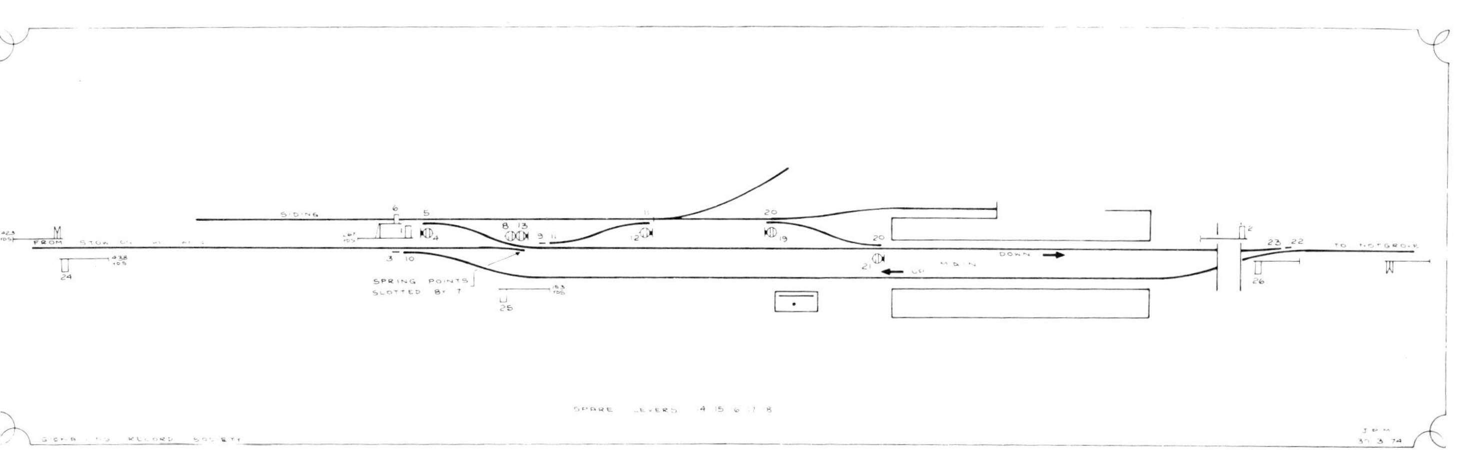

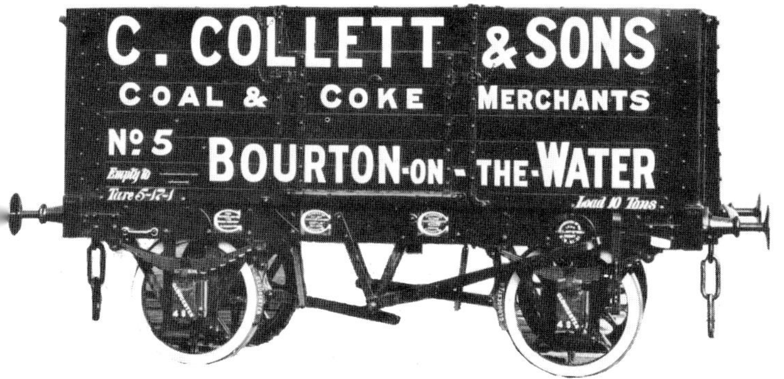

Fig 170

On the Banbury-Cheltenham Branch, after the avoiding loop was built at Kingham, the high spot of the day was naturally the passing of the 'Welsh Express' in both directions. This service was a real 'through' cross-country route. On weekdays, starting from Swansea at 7.40 am, it reached Newcastle at 6.32 pm. The train in the opposite direction leaving Newcastle at 9.30 am, arrived at Swansea at 8.48 pm. (There was a Sunday service which does not concern this book, as it was routed via Oxford and Swindon, the branch being closed to traffic, except for Engineering Department work, on the Sabbath.) The interesting feature, as with all these cross-country trains, was the use of different rolling stock on alternate days. Starting out on Monday from Swansea, the stock would naturally be Great Western origin, whilst the Newcastle train coming down the country would be made up of NER carriages (later LNER). So the two trains made one journey each day all the week, until on the Saturday the GWR stock ended back at Swansea and the North Eastern train returned to Newcastle.

When the service first opened, the train was worked by the 'Duke' class of engine, and the loading was five eight-wheeled stock, but as traffic got heavier, the train was lengthened to eight which included a restaurant car and a 2-6-0 '43XX' class of locomotive was rostered for the service, finally being superseded by the 4-6-0 'Manor' class. Banbury, of course, was the line of demarcation, where the GWR handed over to LNER, and vice versa, and it was here that, not only were the locomotives changed, but also the respective crews and even the train's tail and side lamps. In addition, each train was fully examined by the carriage and wagon examiner and all the carriage numbers were recorded for RCH purposes (one of my many jobs as a lad).

The two pictures on page 92 show both trains. In Figure 170 we see No. 7319 in charge of the LNER train, just approaching Hatherley Curve Junction, prior to running over the Banbury-Cheltenham branch towards Kingham. In the lower illustration, No. 6343 is shown with Great Western stock, running down the incline into Bourton-on-the-Water station. (Figure 171.)

Fig 171

Notgrove

Travelling up this very incline, we continue our survey of the branch, and leaving Bourton-on-the-Water on a single line, again cross both the Windrush and the Fosse Way, heading westwards towards the high Cotswolds. Rising all the way on an average gradient of 1 in 60, first on an embankment and then into a deep cutting, we pass under a high road bridge and enter the left hand platform track at Notgrove station.

Map 25

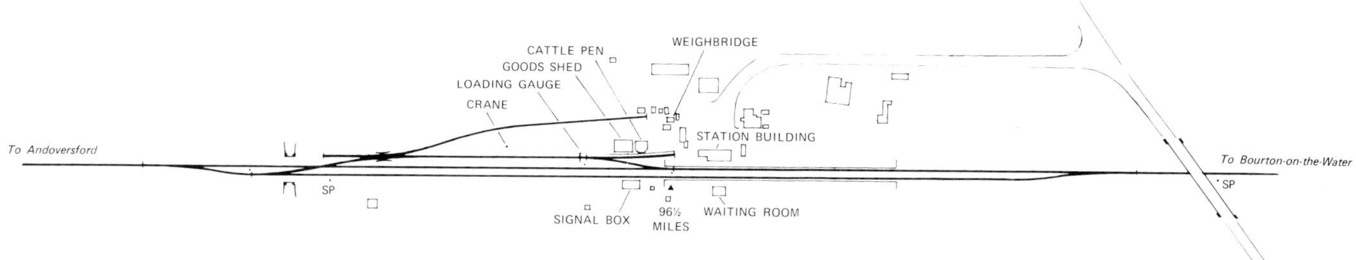

Notgrove

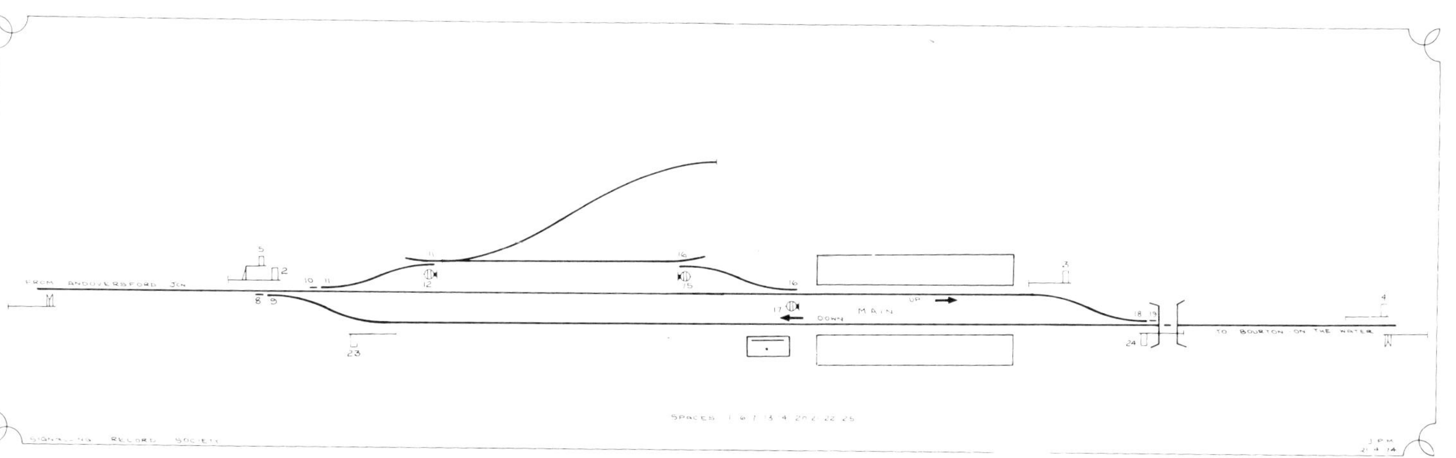

Fig 172

Fig 173

Fig 175

Fig 174

Fig 176

Fig 177

Fig 178

Fig 179

This windswept, small station was noted as being the highest *through* station on the Great Western Railway, topping 760 feet above sea level. Princetown was higher, but this was a single-line terminus station and not a through route. Another of Notgrove's claim to fame was the old Down starting signal, which, like the one at Bourton, was of lattice construction. It can just be seen in Figure 175 (opposite) in a shot I took in 1946. By 1952 it had been changed for a round steel posted variety. (Figure 176 opposite.) In Figure 173 (opposite) the approaching track from Bourton can be seen clearly and such was the gradient that the Up distant signal is within sight of the Down advanced starter!

Looking at the pictures on this page of the main station building, it can be discerned that these were of clapboard construction on to a brick plinth base, with a roof of slates. Cotswold stone predominated, naturally, in the walls and even platforms. One odd feature which I noted was that the chimney breast and chimney were on the platform side of the station office.

Fig 180

Fig 181

On this page, we have two pictures both looking east at Notgrove. The high road bridge can be seen in both, marking the very summit of the climb up from the Windrush in the east and the Coln in the west. In Figure 182, the Up side waiting room can be seen. The similarity with the shelter at Bourton will be noted, except that this building at Notgrove is noticeably higher.

Fig 182

Figure 183 is taken from the end of the Down platform looking west and the rather large red brick signal box is seen on the left, with the black painted wooden goods shed on the right. Notice how the track suddenly drops away downhill just after the loading gauge, and for those interested, the milepost reads 96½ miles from London. In the lower picture, the station buildings are seen again from the low viewpoint of track level, with the Station Master's house directly behind. (Figure 184.)

Fig 183

Fig 184

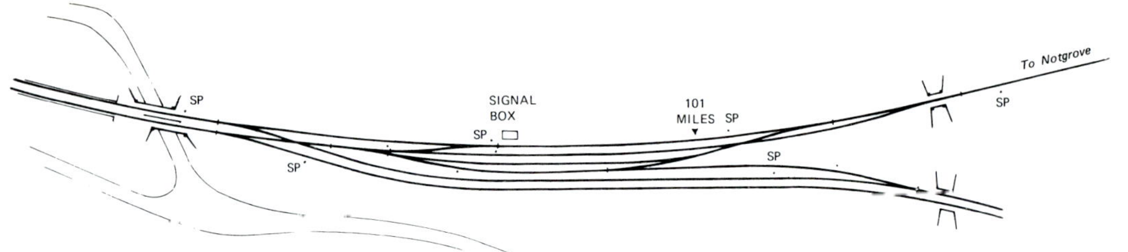

Andoversford Junction & Dowdeswell Sidings

Map 26

Andoversford

In the days when iron ore trains were using this route from the numerous quarries at the eastern end of the line, Notgrove was important. All freight services going west to east had to stop dead there, to allow the wagon brakes to be pinned down and retard the loads on the falling gradients in both directions.

Following on to the west from Notgrove, the single line again passed through solid rock cuttings and hugging the contours of the hills where it could, passed over the Stow-Gloucester road and finally descended to the junction with the Midland and South Western Railway, at what was used to be known as Dowdeswell Sidings. The M & SW Junction line from Andover in the south, through to Swindon and Cirencester in the north, extended its line on from Cirencester to Andoversford Junction in 1891 and, by virtue of running powers granted to them by the GWR, were to work through to Cheltenham. For many years, the M & SW Junction trains called at their own station which was known as Andoversford and Dowdeswell, and it was only later, when these 'foreign' workings were allowed to call at Andoversford station proper, that the junction became known as Andoversford Junction and Dowdeswell Sidings. (See signalling plan and sketch map No. 26.)

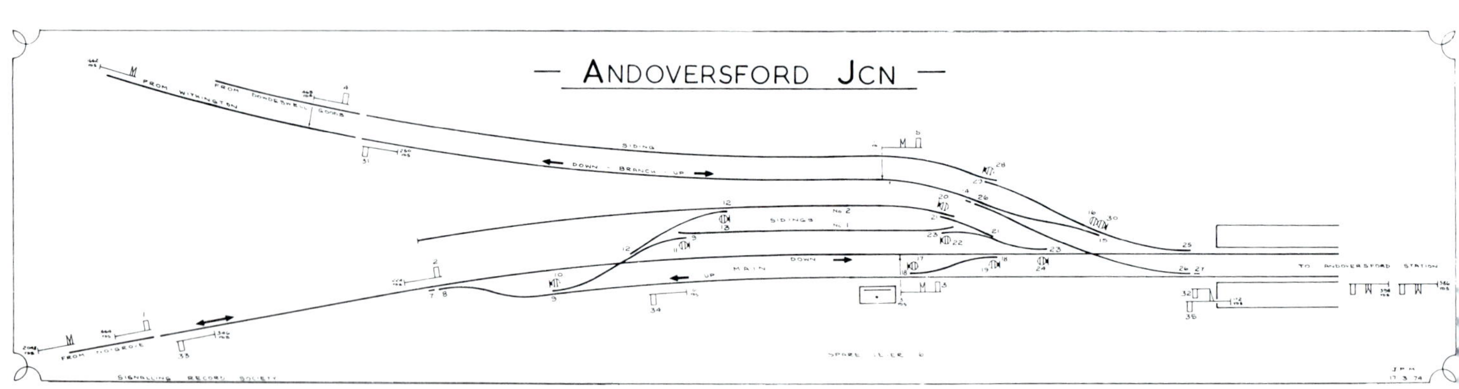

An official view of Gypsy Lane bridge, just east of Andoversford Junction.

Fig 185

Fig 186

Fig 187

The three pictures on this page are all taken from the Down platform at Andoversford looking back east at the junction. The dating, approximately, would be Figure 186 –1930s, Figure 187–1959 and Figure 188–1949.

The road bridge at the end of the platform passed over the main Oxford-Cheltenham A40. The two lines veering away to the right were the M & SW Junction tracks which eventually led to Andover, whilst the double road to the left was over the Banbury-Cheltenham branch which, after passing the junction signal box on the left and the goods sidings on the right, became the single line going off towards Notgrove. In these pictures the passage of time can be seen in the junction home bracket signal; first with the wooden post and arms, and afterwards the steel tubular column and metal arms. Note the growth of the trees at the end of the platform.

Fig 188

Fig 189

Looking westwards, again towards Cheltenham, Figure 189 shows the double lines entering Andoversford station. Incidentally, the whole route from here through to the terminus at St. James was double tracked in 1900. On the left of the photograph is the main station building with its extended platform awning; in the centre, at the end of the Up platform, can be seen Andoversford signal box with the water tower immediately behind and on the right the usual wooden boarded shelter, but this time with a rather overwhelming large flat-topped roof. In the centre illustration, Figure 190, the view is from the opposite end of the platform, facing eastwards again with the buildings showing their westward side. The rectangular brick building on the extreme right was the goods shed and can be seen again in Figure 191. In between this latter building and the station offices was a small corrugated iron structure with a half-round roof which I always assumed was the lamp room, used for the trimming of the station and signal lamps. It can just be discerned in the lower illustration, directly behind the gentleman on the platform. Purists amongst modellers should note that the construction of the two platforms was totally different, that of the Up side being of blue brick and with little or no overlap in places. That on the Down side was of stone blocks with a pronounced bevelled lip, a single line of flagstones, backed by asphalt. However, a close study of these pictures should illustrate these points clearly.

Fig 190

Fig 191

Fig 192

The view in **Figure 192** is that which a driver of a train heading for Cheltenham would have had from the cab of his locomotive. On the left is the Down platform water column, with the starting signal behind, and the loading gauge in the yard is also shown to the left of the running roads. Notice how the double tracks dip and vanish abruptly after passing the outer Home signal, just visible in the centre of the picture. At the right is the all-wooden construction 'Andoversford Station Signal Box' which was painted pale cream when I knew it and directly behind this box is the storage water tank which supplied the platform columns, with its attendant pump house at the base. **Figure 193** is a close-up picture of the Up-side waiting room and shows the building details clearly. Sides and rear were inside framed, whilst the frontage was of the outside-framed style. Three cast-iron brackets sprang from the ends and centre respectively to support that large roof and awning which, incidentally, was leaded. Paintwork was of similar colour to the box, pale primrose cream, with dark buff doors and platform seat.

Fig 193

A final page of details of Andoversford. In Figure 194 the signal box is seen again, but in three-quarter view, which shows the three double sliding windows in the front and the one double similar at each end. The small annexe at the top of the ladder led the way into the cabin from the steps and small platform at first floor level. The ground floor contained all the locking gear and frame, of course, and access to this room was via the small door under the stairway.

The close-up picture on the left is the Down starter at Andoversford and is only included because it was such a typical Great Western signal of the period I knew so well. The wooden arm, red with white stripe, the large spectacles, one red and one a blue colour, which, combined with the yellow flame of the oil lamp, gave a green aspect. The finial had a black square base, a white spike and a red ball with four slots cut therein. The signal had a tapered wooden post with black iron ladder and a small platform for attending to the signal lamp or pivot mechanism. Modellers should note that the arm and spectacles were not conjoined in one piece, but were separated all but for a narrow cast bridge. (Figure 196.)

Finally, a rear view of Andoversford station building, Figure 195, which has had the bricks covered in a cement rendering. The roof was of slate, and the chimneys red brick with biscuit coloured cowls.

Fig 194

Fig 196

Fig 195

Map 27 shows the track layout of Andoversford, followed by the Signal Box Plan

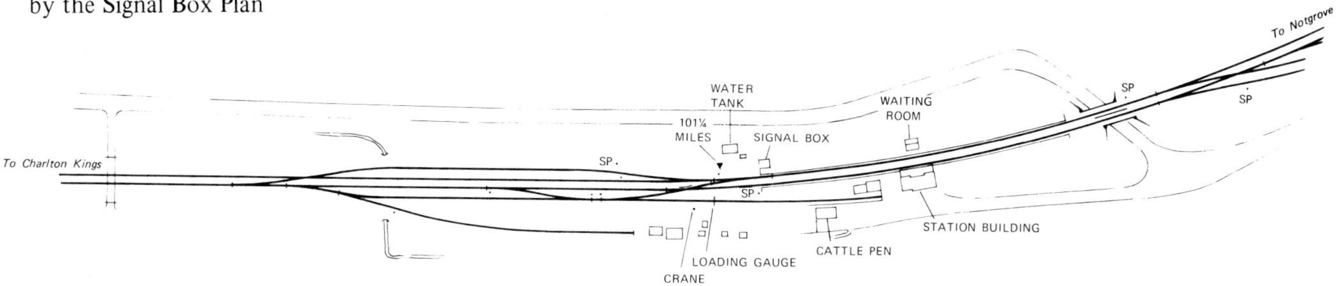

Map 27

Andoversford Station

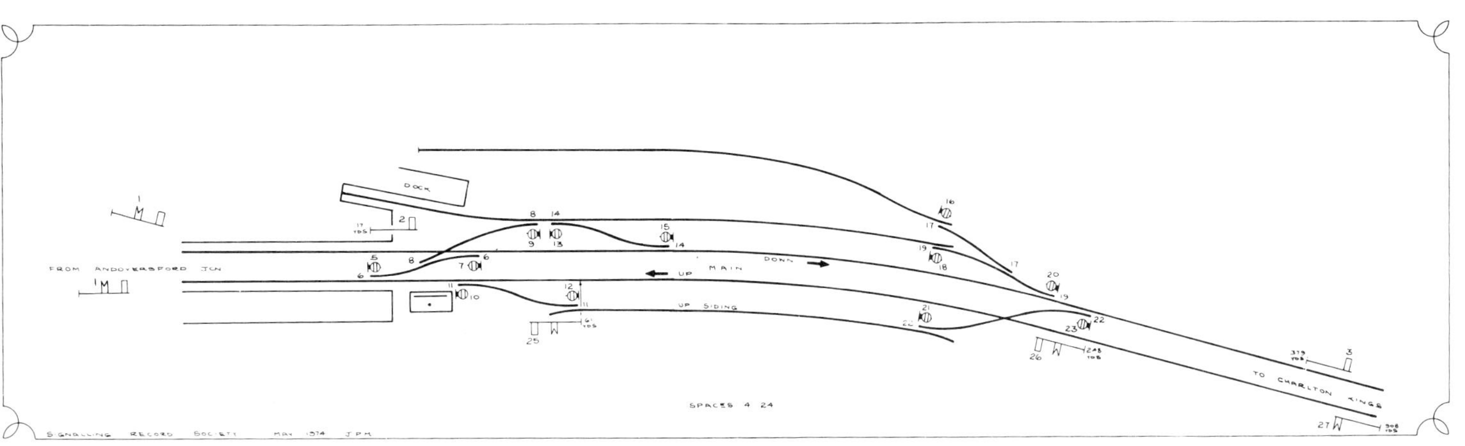

Fig 197

Leaving Andoversford at an altitude of 550 feet, the way to Cheltenham still headed west, but dropped dramatically down on leaving the station, on a descending gradient of 1 in 70! The lines entered into a deep cutting and then, still falling, pierced the high ridge by means of a 400 yard bore, Figure 197, known as 'Sandywell Park Tunnel'. On emerging from this curved underground passage, Figure 198, the line was still in a deep, wooded cutting which quickly gave way to a high embankment, and from there on to a high red brick viaduct of 12 arches. This crossed the ravine of the River Chelt and the small lane running down from the village of Dowdeswell to the A40 trunk road, which followed the railway right down the valley. Figure 199 shows the viaduct from the east, and 200 from the west. Note the new and old piers showing the effect of doubling the line. As the line continued to descend, the scenery improved, a superb view opening out on the right of the series of artificial reservoirs formed by the waters of the Chelt, which act as the drinking water supply for Cheltenham Spa.

Still falling, the branch now entered another wooded cutting and approximately five miles after leaving Andoversford ran into the small station of Charlton Kings.

Fig 198

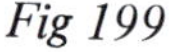

Fig 199

Fig 200

Charlton Kings

This small station had a low timber built structure on the Down side and a waiting room like that at Andoversford on the Up platform, see Figure 190. Up to the late 1930s, a mineral line from the Leckhampton Quarries, 1¼ miles away to the south west, linked up with the branch here, bringing in the limestone traffic for distribution all over the country. Perhaps of note to mention here, the great incline of Leckhampton Hill Quarries, which was of three quarters of a mile in length and rose 450 feet right up to the actual diggings!

When I knew Charlton Kings, all this had gone and the pleasant rural station was prettily set alongside the golf course, with some fine Scots pines growing almost on the platforms! The bridge which carried the A435 from Cheltenham to Cirencester passes over the line just behind the viewpoint seen in **Figure 201**.

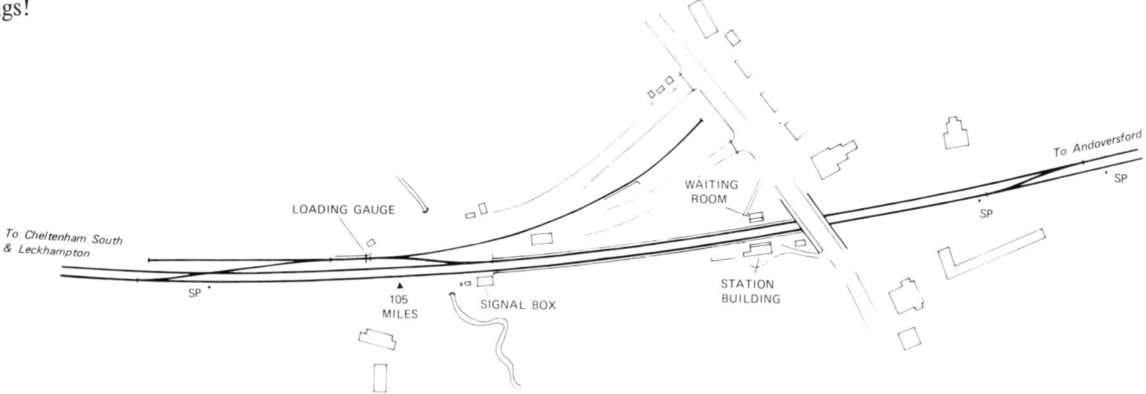

Charlton Kings *Map 28*

Fig 201

Charlton Kings station at 6.40 p.m. on May 19, 1924, flooded after a severe and prolonged thunderstorm during the afternoon.

Fig 202

Fig 203

Fig 204, 14th June, 1923

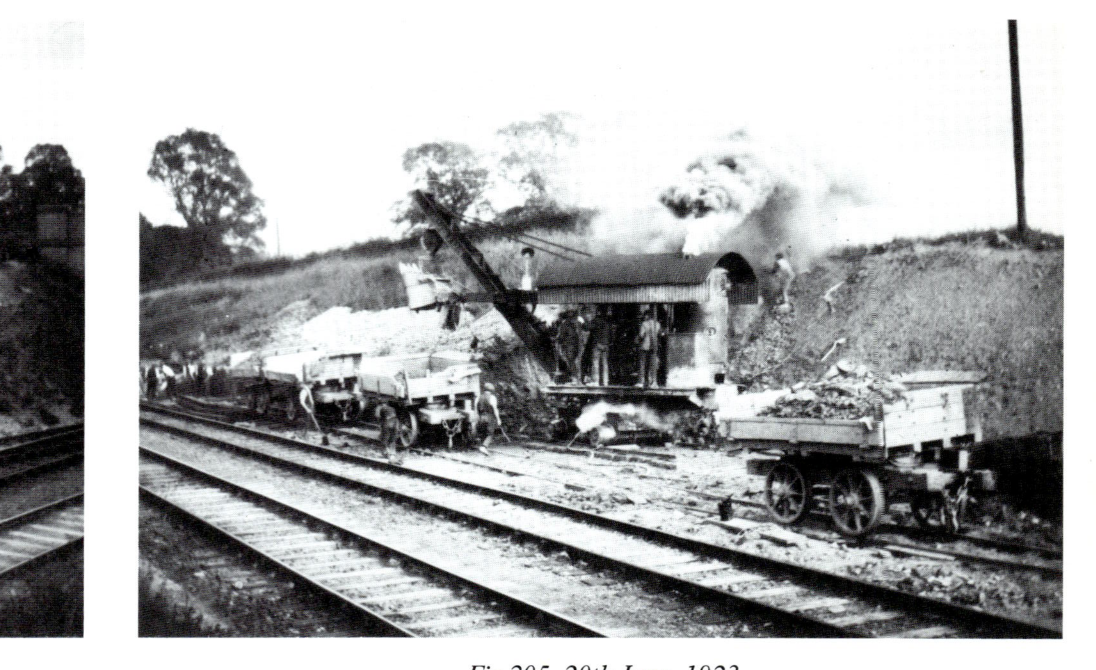

Fig 205, 20th June, 1923

Fig 206, 20th June, 1923

Fig 207, 4th July, 1923

Figures 204-7 were taken at Charlton Kings in 1923 and show a Steam Navvy at work on the construction of the junction between the mineral line from Leckhampton quarries (mentioned on page 106) and the GWR. Figure 208 shows the new trackwork being installed and the final picture in this sequence was taken after the work was completed.

Fig 208, 10th August, 1923

Fig 209, 17th September, 1923

Fig 210

Cheltenham South & Leckhampton

Only one and a half miles from Charlton Kings, and still on a 1 in 77 gradient, the Banbury-Cheltenham line came to the first 'Cheltenhams', in actual fact Leckhampton, but given the extra title 'Cheltenham South', not only to attract traffic from the southern extremity of the town, but also when the through Welsh expresses began to operate, to enable 'Cheltenham' to be added to stations at which the train could call! For instance, when the 3.47 pm 'Barry' express ran into Banbury station, the porters used to call out, 'Cheltenham, Gloucester, Newport, Cardiff and Swansea express' and the Cheltenham they referred to was this Leckhampton stop. Note in these two pictures the length of platform, to accommodate these very trains. Figures 210 and 211 were taken with an interval of some thirty years. Notice how the small conifers on the Down platform have grown into mature trees in this period of time. Incidentally, both these views are looking east towards Kingham, Figure 210 being taken from the overbridge, featured in Figure 212, taking the B4070 to Birdlip. One feature always impressed itself upon me, the likeness of Leckhampton station building with that of Chipping Norton.

Fig 211

Fig 212

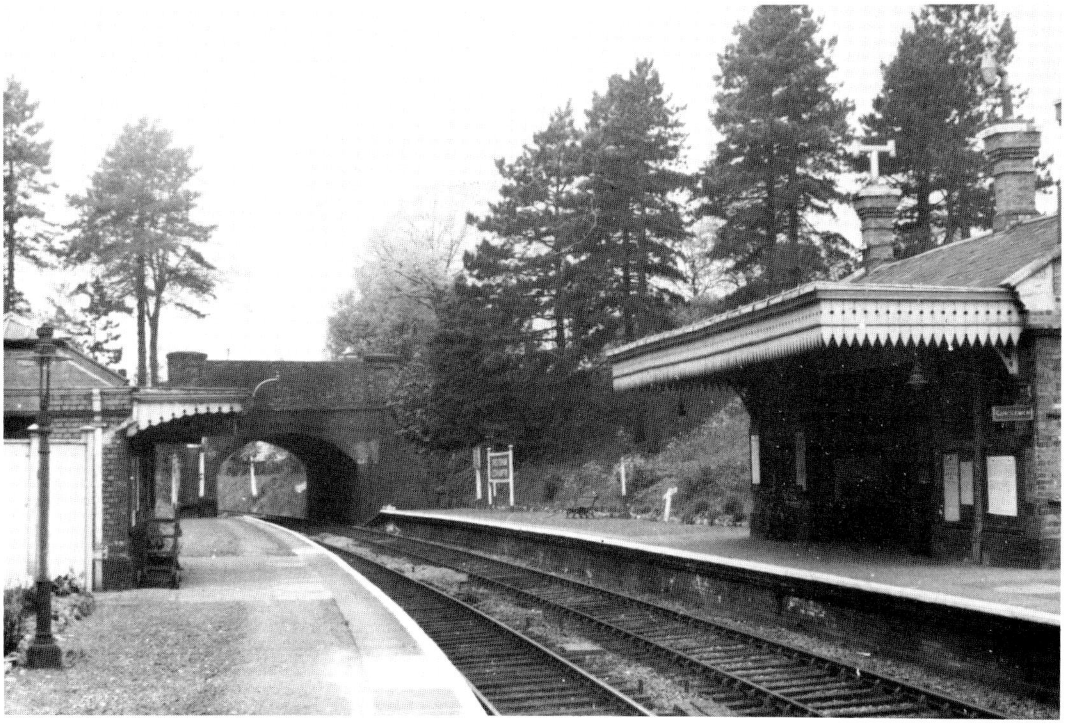

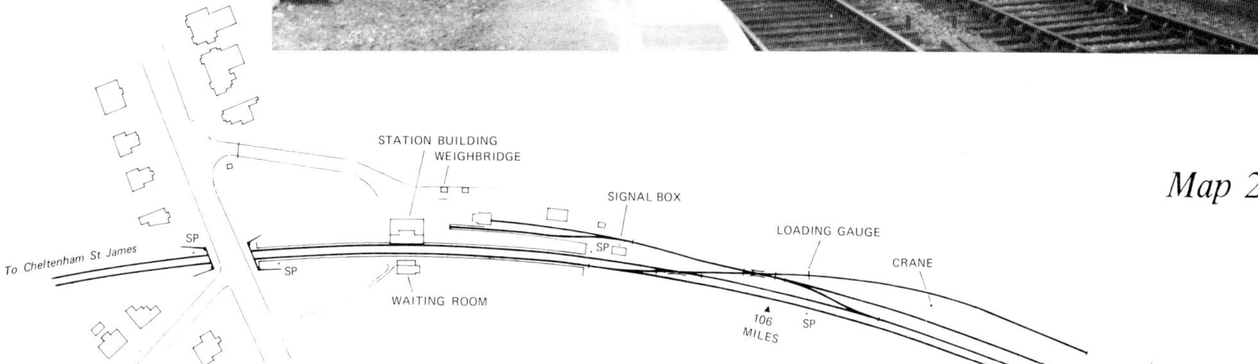

Map 29

STATION BUILDING
WEIGHBRIDGE
SIGNAL BOX
LOADING GAUGE
CRANE
To Cheltenham St James
SP
SP
SP
WAITING ROOM
106 MILES
SP
SP
To Charlton Kings

Cheltenham South & Leckhampton

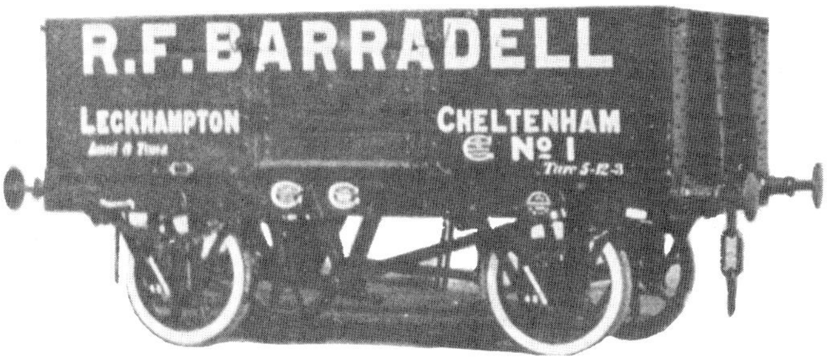

R.F. BARRADELL
LECKHAMPTON
CHELTENHAM
No 1

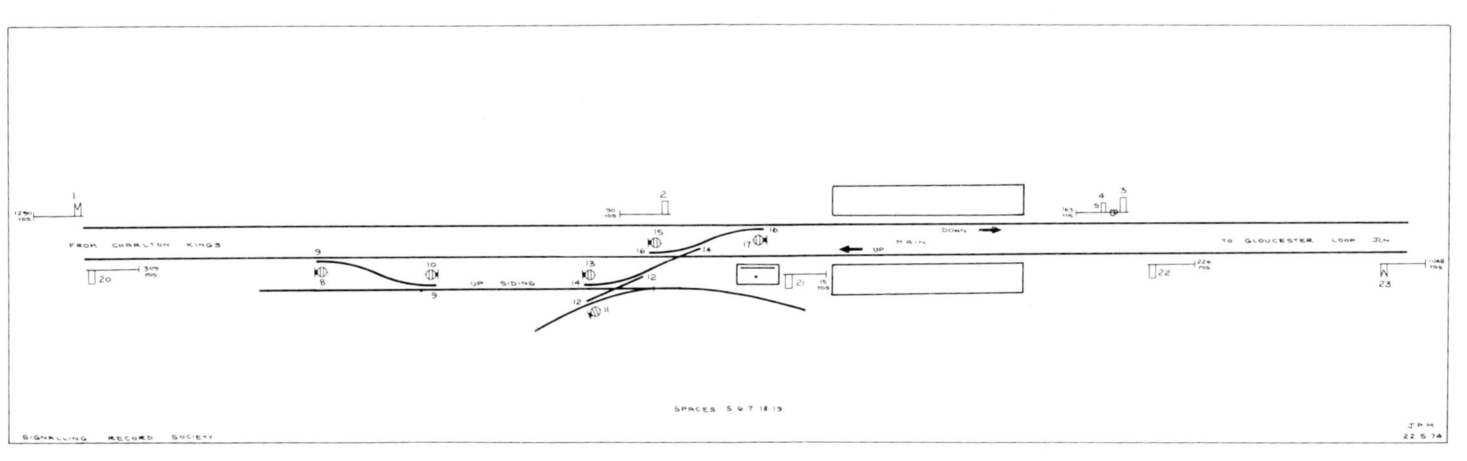

Getting close to our destination now, we come to the first of what used to be three double line junctions set in the form of a triangle. The top picture shows all that was left of Gloucester Loop Junction in 1959. Trains for Gloucester would take the left-hand tracks, whilst those for Cheltenham would veer off to the right through Banbury Line Junction, right handed again at Lansdown Junction into Cheltenham Malvern Road and finally on to the terminus at Cheltenham St. James.

Just for interest's sake, Figure 214 illustrates Hatherley Curve Junction, the other end of the Gloucester road loop. Figure 215 shows the LMS Lansdown station and lines on the left, with Honeybourne tracks on the right. The lower picture is of Lansdown Line Junction. (Figure 216.)

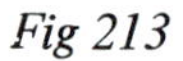

Fig 213

Fig 214

Fig 215

Fig 216

Map 30

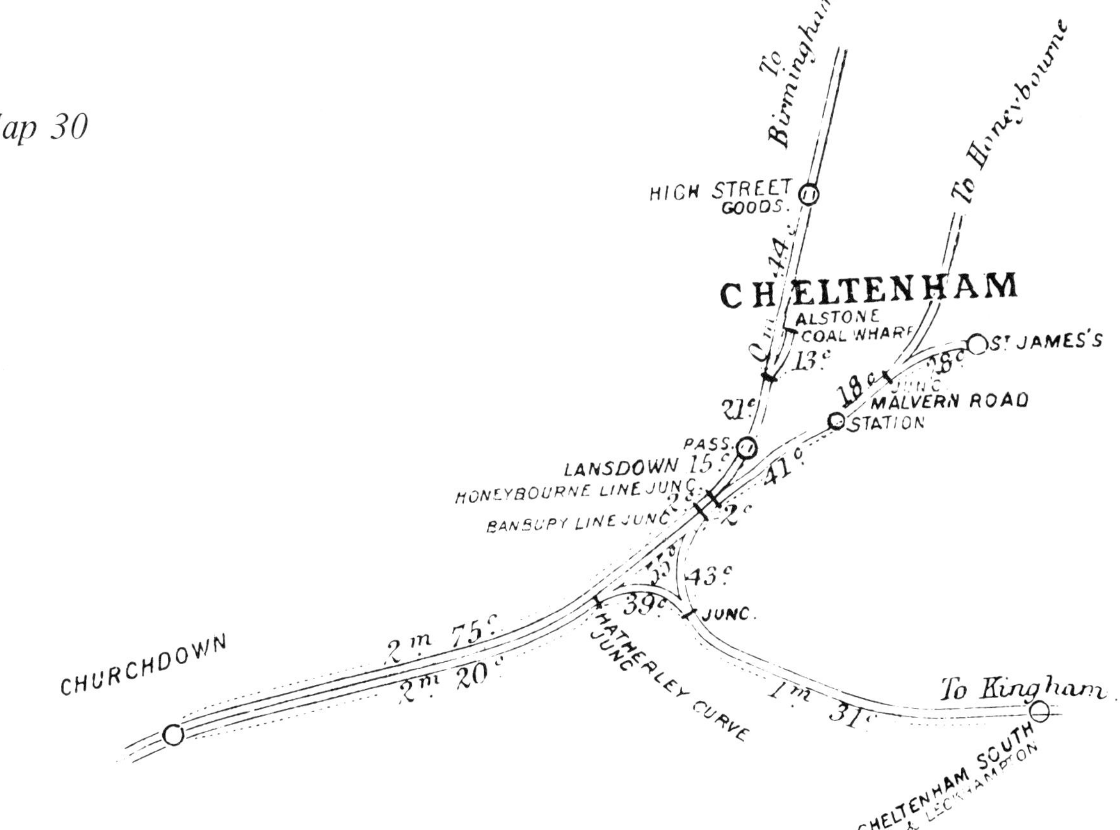

This early view of Lansdown Junction makes an interesting comparison with the previous view.

Fig 217

Fig 218

Cheltenham Malvern Road

The various tracks, routes and stations in the Cheltenham area were many and various, so to attempt a clarification I add a small sketch plan of the layout, which I hope will show the geographical position of the junctions and depots. (See Map 30.)

Passing over the Gloucester Loop Junction, our imaginary journey negotiates a severe right handed curve, where we change directions from westward to eastward, join the LMS and GWR joint lines at Banbury Line Junction, take the right-hand bearing at Honeybourne Line Junction fork, and arrives in Cheltenham (Malvern Road) Station. (Figures 218 and 219.)

This station was built on the opening of the Gloucester-Honeybourne-Birmingham line in 1908 and at the east end of the layout we again bear right away from the West Midland line into the terminus of Cheltenham St. James.

Fig 219

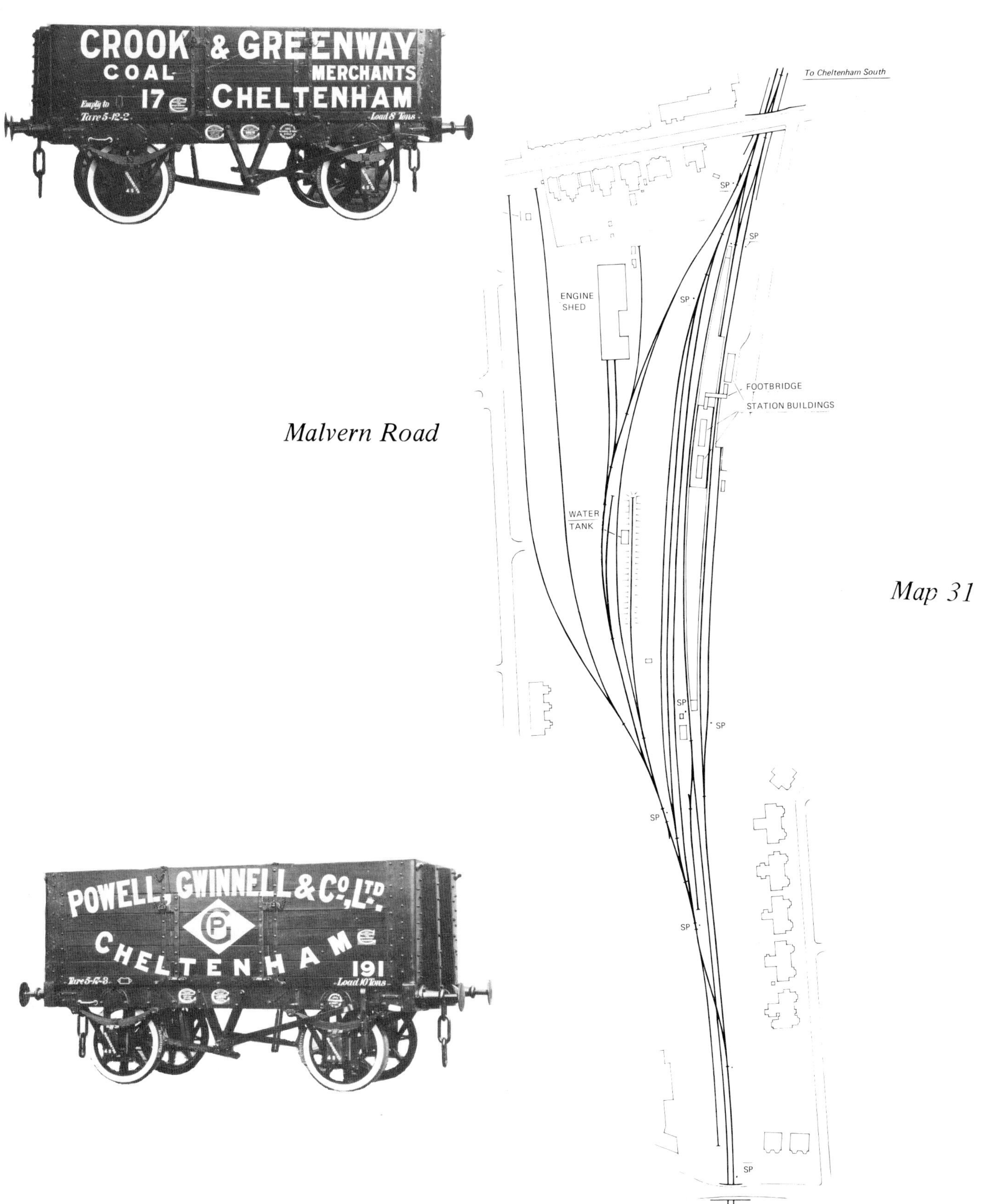
CROOK & GREENWAY
COAL MERCHANTS
Empty to 17
CHELTENHAM
Tare 5-12-2
Load 8 Tons
POWELL, GWINNELL & Co. LTD
CHELTENHAM
191
Tare 5-12-3
Load 10 Tons
To Cheltenham South
SP
ENGINE SHED
FOOTBRIDGE
STATION BUILDINGS
WATER TANK
To Cheltenham St. James

Malvern Road

Map 31

Fig 220

Fig 221

Cheltenham St. James

Fig 222

Fig 223

This large station takes its name from St. James Square adjacent and consists of two long semi-island platforms joined at the road end by a large circulating area. Figures 222 and 223 illustrate St. James looking towards the buffer stops and in the left hand platform road, (Figure 222) can be seen the Kingham branch train, awaiting the 'right away' over the very line which we have in these few pages made our journey. Figure 224 completes this section and shows the fine exterior to this station.

Fig 224

Map 32

An early track plan of Cheltenham St James.

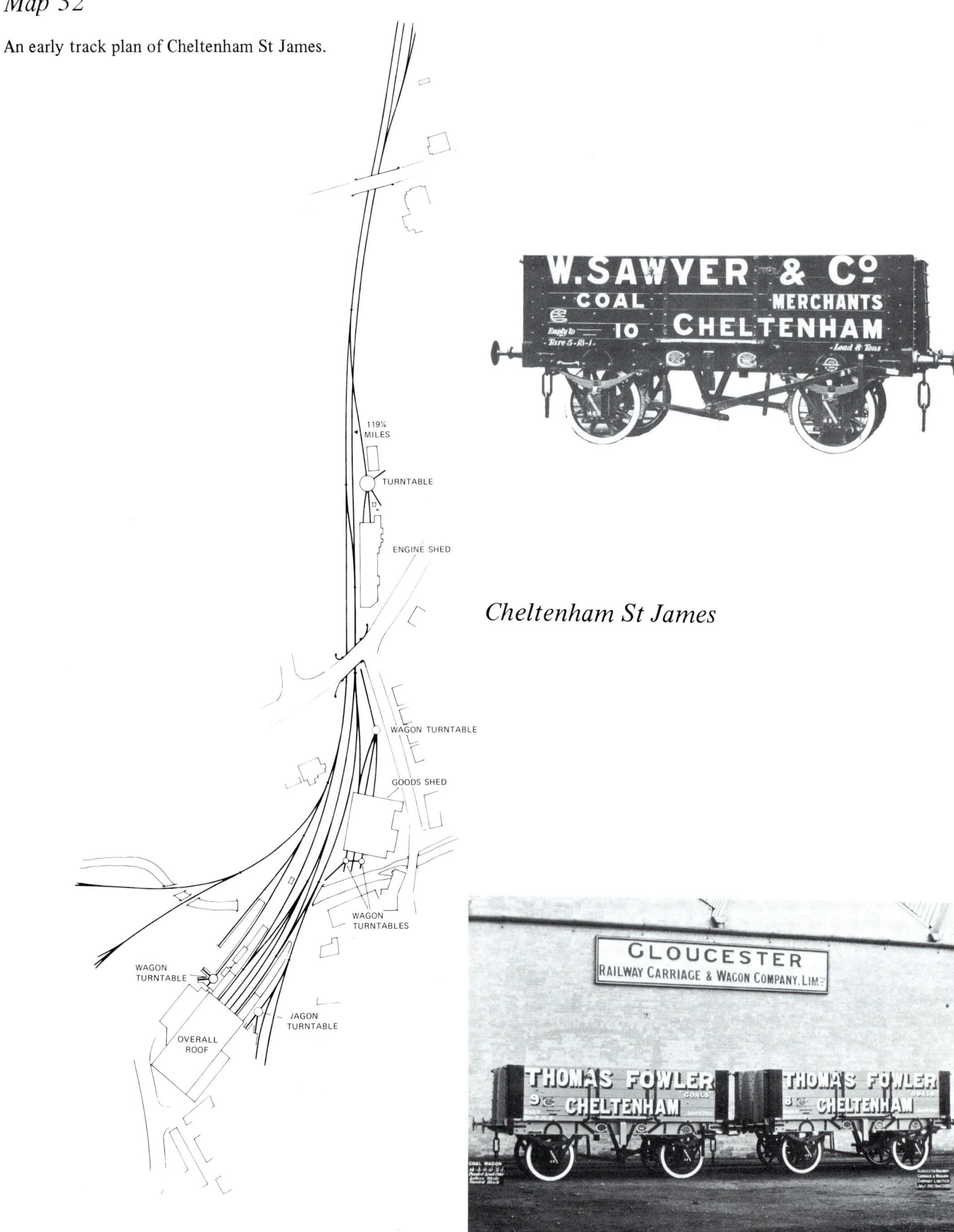

Cheltenham St James

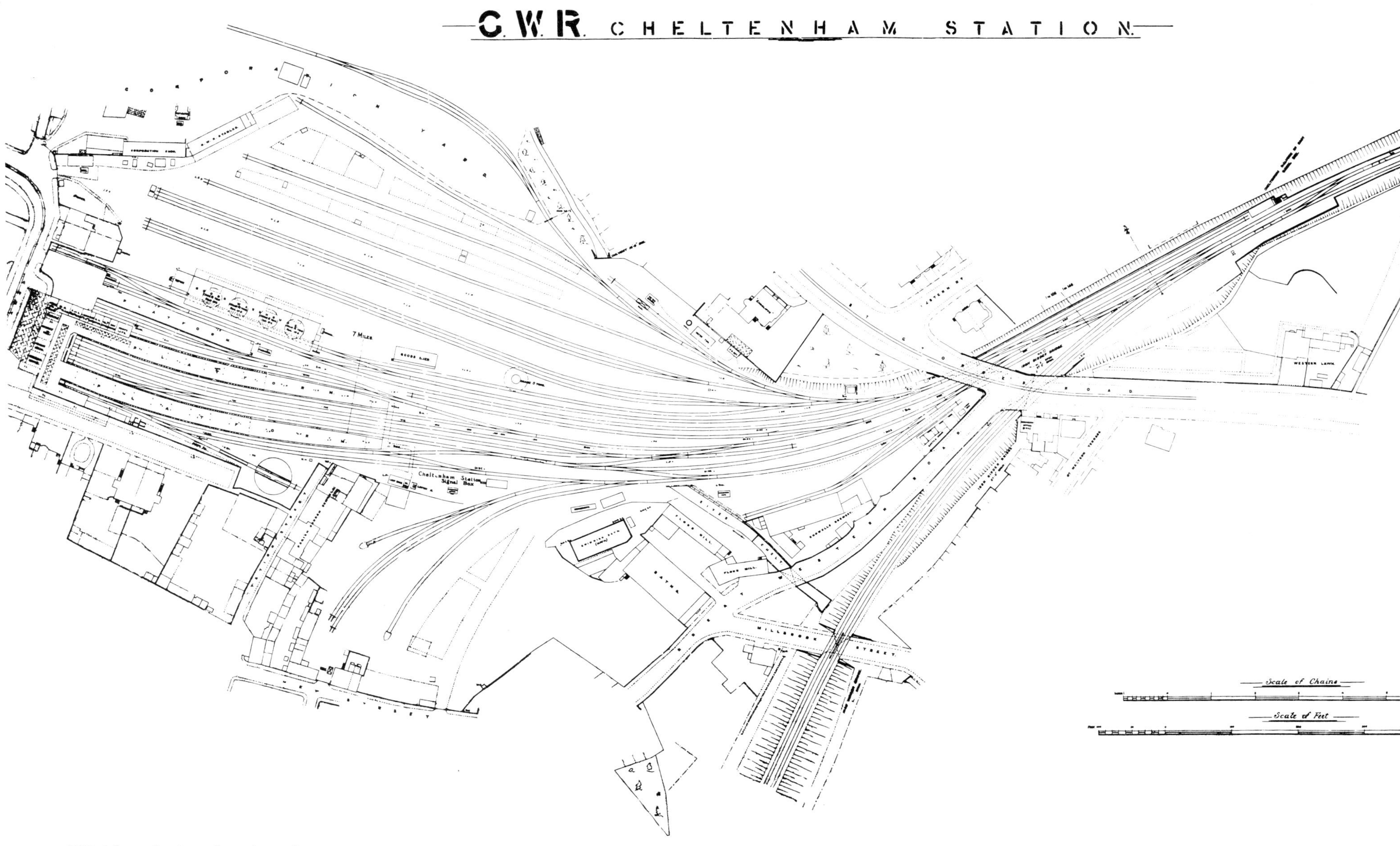

Official track plan after alterations.

Fig 225

Fig 226

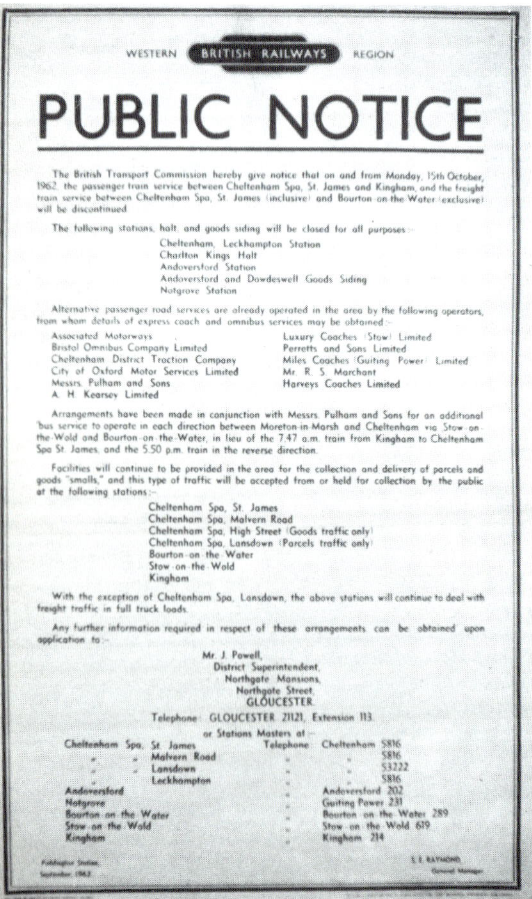

WESTERN BRITISH RAILWAYS REGION

PUBLIC NOTICE

The British Transport Commission hereby give notice that on and from Monday, 15th October, 1962, the passenger train service between Cheltenham Spa, St. James and Kingham, and the freight train service between Cheltenham Spa, St. James (inclusive) and Bourton-on-the-Water (exclusive) will be discontinued.

The following stations, halt, and goods siding will be closed for all purposes:–

Cheltenham, Leckhampton Station
Charlton Kings Halt
Andoversford Station
Andoversford and Dowdeswell Goods Siding
Notgrove Station

Alternative passenger road services are already operated in the area by the following operators, from whom details of express coach and omnibus services may be obtained:–

Associated Motorways	Luxury Coaches (Stow) Limited
Bristol Omnibus Company Limited	Perretts and Sons Limited
Cheltenham District Traction Company	Miles Coaches (Guiting Power) Limited
City of Oxford Motor Services Limited	Mr. R. S. Marchant
Messrs. Pulham and Sons	Harveys Coaches Limited
A. H. Kearsey Limited	

Arrangements have been made in conjunction with Messrs. Pulham and Sons for an additional 'bus service to operate in each direction between Moreton-in-Marsh and Cheltenham via Stow-on-the-Wold and Bourton-on-the-Water, in lieu of the 7.47 a.m. train from Kingham to Cheltenham Spa St. James, and the 5.50 p.m. train in the reverse direction.

Facilities will continue to be provided in the area for the collection and delivery of parcels and goods "smalls," and this type of traffic will be accepted from or held for collection by the public at the following stations:–

Cheltenham Spa, St. James
Cheltenham Spa, Malvern Road
Cheltenham Spa, High Street (Goods traffic only)
Cheltenham Spa, Lansdown (Parcels traffic only)
Bourton-on-the-Water
Stow-on-the-Wold
Kingham

With the exception of Cheltenham Spa, Lansdown, the above stations will continue to deal with freight traffic in full truck loads.

Any further information required in respect of these arrangements can be obtained upon application to:–

Mr. J. Powell,
District Superintendent,
Northgate Mansions,
Northgate Street,
GLOUCESTER.

Telephone: GLOUCESTER 21121, Extension 113.

or Stations Masters at:–

Cheltenham Spa,	St. James	Telephone	Cheltenham 5816
" "	Malvern Road	"	" 5816
" "	Lansdown	"	" 53222
"	Leckhampton	"	" 5816
Andoversford		"	Andoversford 202
Notgrove		"	Guiting Power 231
Bourton-on-the-Water		"	Bourton-on-the-Water 289
Stow-on-the-Wold		"	Stow-on-the-Wold 619
Kingham		"	Kingham 214

Paddington Station,
September 1962

S. E. RAYMOND,
General Manager

Fig 227

Finally, just to record the other station at Cheltenham, two pictures of the ex-LMS building at Lansdown, one taken from the platforms inside and the other from the outside approach, showing the colonnaded concourse and taxi rank of the 1930's.

The last sad illustration is the proclamation of September 1962, issued by British Railways, decreeing that as and from 15th October 1962, all passenger and freight service over the Banbury-Cheltenham branch would cease. *Tempus edax rerum.*

Timetables

1883

BANBURY AND CHELTENHAM RAILWAY.

STATIONS.	WEEK DAYS. a.m.	a.m.	p.m.	p.m.	p.m.	STATIONS.	WEEK DAYS. a.m.	a.m.	a.m.	p.m.	p.m.
Chipping Norton Jun.	8 50	9 42	1 0	5 24	8 58	Cheltenham	6 50	10 0	11 20	3 15	6 50
Stow-on-the-Wold ...	9 0	9 52	1 10	5 34	9 8	Leckhampton	6 59	10 9	11 29	3 24	6 59
Bourton-on-Water ...	9 8	10 0	1 20	5 42	9 16	Charlton Kings	7 4	10 14	11 34	3 29	7 4
Notgrove & Westfield	9 20	10 12	1 33	5 57	9 28	Andoversford	7 14	10 25	11 44	3 39	7 14
Andoversford	9 33	10 25	1 46	6 11	9 39	Notgrove & Westfield	7 25	10 36	11 55	3 50	7 25
Charlton Kings.........	9 44	10 36	1 58	6 23	9 49	Bourton-on-Water ...	7 37	10 48	12 7	4 2	7 37
Leckhampton	9 51	10 42	2 5	6 29	9 55	Stow-on-the-Wold ...	7 45	10 55	12 15	4 10	7 45
Cheltenham	10 0	10 50	2 15	6 39	10 2	Chipping Norton Jun.	7 55	11 5	12 25	4 20	7 55

1902

BANBURY AND CHELTENHAM.

Down Trains.		Week Days only. a.m.	a.m.	a.m.	p.m.	p.m.	p.m.	p.m.
London (Paddington)	dep	...	...	7 25	...	12 15	4 J55	...
Reading	,,	.	.	8 40	.	1 15	4 J35	.
Oxford	,,	...	...	10 10	...	2 13	6 J28	...
Banbury	arr	.	.	10 40	.	2 43	.	.
Birmingham	dep	...	...	9 25	...	1 5	5 45	...
Leamington	,,	.	.	10 10	.	2 14	6 18	.
Banbury	arr	...	...	10 55	...	3 0	6 45	...
Banbury	dep	7 0	.	11 15	.	3 25	7 15	.
King's Sutton	,,	7 8	...	11 23	...	3 33	7 23	...
Adderbury	,,	7 13	.	11 28	.	3 38	7 28	.
Bloxham	,,	7 20	...	11 35	...	3 45	7 35	...
Hook Norton	,,	7 31	.	11 47	.	3 56	7 46	.
Chipping Norton	arr	7 44	...	12 0	...	4 9	7 59	...
	dep	7 46	8 30	12 10	3 15	4 10	8 0	9 0
Chipping Norton Junction	arr	7 55	8 40	12 20	3 25	4 20	8 10	9 10
Chipping Norton Junction	dep	8 5	.	12 44	3 48	4 40	8 19	.
Oxford	arr	8 49	...	1 10	4 15	5 30	9 5	...
Reading	,,	9 43	.	2 45	5 0	6 27	9 58	.
London (Paddington) ...	,,	10 25	...	2 33	5 50	7 32	10 50	...
Chipping Norton Junction	dep	.	8 53	12 46	3 37	4 35	.	9 30
Evesham	arr	...	9 46	1 40	4 12	5 35	...	10 11
Worcester (Shrub Hill) .	,,	.	10 22	2 14	4 36	6 10	.	10 36
London (Paddington) ...	dep	...	5 40	9 45	1 45	1 50	...	6 50
Reading	,,	.	6 42	10 58	1 15	2 55	.	7 43
Oxford	,,	...	7 58	11 55	3 8	3 42	...	8 43
Chipping Norton Junction	arr	.	8 50	12 42	3 34	4 30	.	9 27
Chipping Norton Junction	dep	...	8 58	1 5	3 40	5 0	...	9 40
Stow-on-the-Wold	,,	.	9 7	1 16	.	5 9	.	9 49
Bourton-on-the-Water	,,	...	9 13	1 24	3 58	5 17	...	9 55
Notgrove	,,	.	9 27	1 39	.	5 31	.	10 9
Andoversford	,,	...	9 37	1 51	...	5 42	...	10 19
Charlton Kings	,,	.	9 44	2 1	.	5 51	.	10 26
Leckhampton	,,	...	9 50	2 8	...	5 58	...	10 33
Cheltenham . .	arr	.	9 57	2 17	4 30	6 5	.	10 40
Cheltenham	dep	...	10 10	2 52	5 20	6 20	...	11 30
Gloucester	arr	.	10 25	3 7	5 37	6 37	.	11 45

Up Trains.		Week Days only. a.m.	a.m.	a.m.		p.m.	p.m.	
Gloucester	dep	...	9 25	10 40	...	2 38	6 36	...
Cheltenham	arr	.	9 45	11 0	.	2 53	6 55	.
Cheltenham	dep	6 50	10 20	11 40	...	3 10	7 5	...
Leckhampton	,,	6 59	10 28	.	.	3 19	7 15	.
Charlton Kings.............	,,	7 4	10 33	...	...	3 24	7 20	...
Andoversford	,,	7 14	10 43	.	.	3 34	7 30	.
Notgrove	,,	7 25	10 55	...	...	3 45	7 41	...
Bourton-on-the-Water . . .	,,	7 36	11 7	12 15	.	4 0	7 51	.
Stow-on-the-Wold	,,	7 42	11 13	...	...	4 6	7 57	...
Chipping Norton Junction	arr	7 50	11 22	12 27	.	4 14	8 5	.
Chipping Norton Junction	dep	8 5	11 48	12 44	...	4 40	8 19	...
Oxford	arr	8 49	12 36	1 10	.	5 30	9 5	.
Reading	,,	9 43	1 30	2 45	...	6 27	9 58	...
London (Paddington) .	,,	10 25	2 10	2 33	.	7 32	10 50	.
Worcester (Shrub Hill) ...	dep	6 45	10 10	11 30	...	3 0	6 40	...
Evesham	,,	7 11	10 46	11 56	.	3 34	7 15	.
Chipping Norton Junction	arr	8 0	11 43	12 34	...	4 33	8 13	...
London (Paddington) .	dep	.	9 50	.	.	1 50	4 55	.
Reading	,,	...	10 0	10 58	...	2 55	4 35	...
Oxford	,,	.	11 20	11 55	.	3 42	6 35	.
Chipping Norton Junction	arr	...	11 48	12 42	...	4 30	7 25	...
Chipping Norton Junction	dep	8 10	12 0	1 D10	.	4 49	8 35	.
Chipping Norton . .	arr	8 19	12 9	1 D25	...	4 58	8 44	...
	dep	8 20	12 11		.	5 0	8 45	.
Hook Norton	,,	8 34	12 25	...	...	5 14	8 59	...
Bloxham	,,	8 42	12 33	.	.	5 23	9 7	.
Adderbury	,,	8 48	12 40	...	...	5 30	9 13	...
King's Sutton	,,	8 53	12 45	.	.	5 35	9 18	.
Banbury	arr	9 0	12 52	...	...	5 42	9 25	...
Banbury	dep	9 17	1 17	.	.	5 58	.	.
Leamington	arr	9 45	2 0	...	...	6 26	...	...
Birmingham	,,	10 34	3 47	.	.	7 14	.	.
Banbury	dep	10 55	1 25	...	...	..	...	...
Oxford	arr	11 47	1 57	.	.	6 R45	.	.
Reading	,,	12 55	2 45	...	...	8 R0	...	...
London (Paddington) . .	,,	1 58	3 30	.	.	8 R45	.	.

D—Mixed Train. J—Change at King's Sutton for Banbury and Cheltenham Line. R—Change at King's Sutton from Banbury and Cheltenham Line.

ROUTES FOR RETURN TICKETS. For particulars, see page 166.

CHIPPING NORTON BRANCH.

Week Days only.		a.m.	Mxd a.m.	a.m.	noon	Mxd p.m.	p.m.	p.m.	p.m.	p.m.	p.m.
Chipping Norton Junction	dep	8 10	9 10	10 20	12 0	1 10	3 55	4 49	6 45	8 35	9 35
Chipping Norton	arr	8 19	9 30	10 30	12 9	1 25	4 5	4 58	6 55	8 44	9 45

		a.m.	a.m.	a.m.	Mxd a.m.	p.m.		p.m.	p.m.	Mxd p.m.	p.m.	p.m.
Chipping Norton	dep	7 46	8 30	9 55	11 25	12 10	...	3 15	4 10	6 10	8 0	9 0
Chipping Norton Junction	arr	7 55	8 40	10 5	11 40	12 20	.	3 25	4 20	6 25	8 10	9 10

1944

90 BANBURY, CHIPPING NORTON AND CHELTENHAM SPA.

(Third class only between Banbury and Kingham.)

Week Days only.		a.m.	a.m.	a.m.	a.m.	p.m.	p.m.	p.m.	p.m.	p.m.	p.m.	p.m.
Banbury	dep.	6 20			10 55			3 50			7 50	
King's Sutton	,,	6 29			11 3			3 58			7 58	
Adderbury	,,	6 36			11 9			4 4			8 3	
Milton Halt	,,	6 42			11 13			4 8			A	
Bloxham	,,	6 48			11 19			4 14			8 10	
Hook Norton	,,	6 58			11 28			4 23			8 20	
Rollright Halt	,,	7 7			11 37			4 32			8 29	
Chipping Norton	arr.	7 13			11 43		X	4 38			8 35	
	dep.	7 17			11 45		3 40	4 40			8 40	
Sarsden Halt	,,	7 24			11 50		3 45	4 45			8 45	
Kingham	arr.	7 29			11 55		3 50	4 50			8 50	
Kingham	dep.		9 5			12 32			5 15			9 0
Stow-on-the-Wold	,,		9 14			12 42			5 24			9 9
Bourton-on-the-Water	,,		9 20			12 51			5 30			9 14
Notgrove	,,		9 31			1 3			5 40			9 25
Andoversford Junction	,,		9 40	10 45		1 15			5 53	8 20		9 33
Charlton Kings	,,		9 47	10 52		1 22			6 0			9 40
Cheltenham (South) & Leckhampton	,,		9 50	10 56		1 25			6 3	8 30		9 45
Cheltenham Spa (Malvern Road)	,,		9 56			1 33			6 10			
Cheltenham Spa (St. James')	arr.		9 58			1 35			6 12			9 53

		a.m.	a.m.	a.m.	a.m.	p.m.	p.m.	p.m.	p.m.	p.m.	p.m.	p.m.	p.m.
Cheltenham Spa (St James')	dep.	6 32			10 55			2 45			7 5		
Cheltenham Spa (Malvern Road)	,,				10 58			2 48			7 8		
Cheltenham (South) & Leckhampton	,,	6 39		10 30	11 4			2 54	3 26		7 15	7 46	
Charlton Kings	,,	6 44		10 35	11 9			2 59	3 31		7 20	7 52	
Andoversford Junction	,,	6 53		10 45	11 18			3 9	3 40		7 28	8 1	
Notgrove	,,	7 4			11 29			3 18			7 39		
Bourton-on-the-Water	,,	7 13			11 38			3 28			7 50		
Stow-on-the-Wold	,,	7 20			11 42			3 34			7 57		
Kingham	arr.	7 30			11 52		X	3 43			8 7		
Kingham	dep.		7 50			12 30	3 15			5 10			9 20
Sarsden Halt	,,		7 55			12 35	3 21			5 16			9 26
Chipping Norton	arr		8 1			12 41	3 27			5 22			9 33
	dep.		8 2			12 46				5 25			9 37
Rollright Halt	,,		8 8			12 52				5 31			9 44
Hook Norton	,,		8 16			1 0				5 39			9 52
Bloxham	,,		8 25			1 10				5 49			10 3
Milton Halt	,,		8 29			1 14				5 53			10 9
Adderbury	,,		8 33			1 19				5 58			10 16
King's Sutton	,,		8 38			1 24				6 3			
Banbury	arr.		8 44			1 30				6 9			10 30

196 BANBURY, CHIPPING NORTON, AND CHELTENHAM SPA.

Week Days.

Miles																							
			a.m.	a.m.	a.m.	a.m.	a.m.	a.m.	a.m.	a.m.	a.m.	p.m.	p.m.	p.m.	a.m.	p.m.	p.m.	p.m.		p.m.	p.m.	p.m.	p.m.
								Mondays, Thursdays and Saturdays only.						Through Carriages London to Chelt. Spa.		Thurs. and Sats. only.			Through Restaurant Car Train Newcastle-on-Tyne to Cardiff, Barry and Swansea.			Saturdays only.	
.	**London** (Paddington)	dep	1 30	.	5 30	.	.	*5 45*	.	9C10	.	.	.		11C15	.	.	.		2C10	.	.	.
...	Oxford	„	*2A10*	...	7 20	...	...	...	...	9J40	10 15	...	...		12 55	...	...	2 35		2 35	3 30	...	...
—	**Banbury**	dep	6M20	.	8 17	.	.	*9 16*	.	10M35	11 10	.	.		1 56	.	.	3 37		4M3	4 30	.	.
3½	King's Sutton	„	6 29	...	...	...	...	...	...	10 43	...	...	...		...	...	...	...		4 11	...	...	...
5¼	Adderbury	„	6 35	.	R	.	.	R	.	10 49	R	.	.		R	.	.	.		4 17	R	.	.
6¾	Milton Halt	„	6 42	...	...	...	...	...	...	10 52	...	...	...		...	...	...	...		4 21	...	...	...
8¼	Bloxham	„	6 48	.	8‡30	.	.	*9‡31*	.	10 57	11‡23	.	.		2‡9	.	.	.		4 26	4‡43	.	.
12½	Hook Norton	„	6 58	...	...	...	...	*9‡52*	...	11 7	...	...	...		...	...	...	...		4 36	...	...	...
16¼	Rollright Halt	„	7 7	.	.	.	R	*10‡3*	R	11 16	.	.	R		...	☞	R	.		4 45	.	☞	R
19	Chipping Norton	arr	7 13	...	8d58	...	...	*10 15*	...	11 22	11d51	...	...		2d37	...	...	N		4 51	5d11	...	...
		dep	7 16	8d0	STOP	9 35	9d40		11d15	11 24	...	12 50	1d50		...	*3 15*	4d10	.		4 54	STOP	*6 25*	6d30
21¾	Sarsden Halt	„	7 22	R		9 40	...		...	11 29	..	12 55	...		...	*3 20*	...	...		4 59	...	*6 30*	...
23¾	**Kingham**	arr	7 29	8 20	.	9 45	10 0	☞	11 36	11 34	.	1 0	2 11		.	*3 25*	4 30	.		5 4	.	*6 35*	6 53
—	Oxford	arr	8 30	STOP	...	10 42	10 42		12 38	12 38	...	1 39	STOP	☞	...	*4 10*	5 35	...		7 21	...	*7 21*	7 35
—	**London** (Paddington)	„	9 50	a.m.	.	12 5	12 5		2X10	2X10	.	3Y0	a.m.		.	*5 50*	7 28	.		9Y20	p.m.	*9Y20*	9Y20
—	**London** (Paddington)	dep	...	5 30	...	...	...						9 45	12U45	...	...	...	...		STOP	1Y45	...	STOP
—	Oxford	„	.	7 37	.	.	...						11g32	*1b15*	...	.	.	...		.	3 50	.	.
—	**Kingham**	dep	...	8 38	...	...	...						1 20	2 22	...	...	...	...		...	5 10	...	...
28	Stow-on-the-Wold	„	.	8 47	.	.	...						1 29	2 30	...	.	.	B		.	5 19	.	.
30	Bourton-on-the-Water	„	...	8 53	...	...	...						1 34	2 36	...	...	...	L		...	5 24	...	...
35	Notgrove	„	.	9 4	a.m.	.	.						1 45	V	.	.	.	.		p.m.	5 35	.	p.m.
39¾	Andoversford Junction	„	...	9 13	10 37	...	...						1 53	2 57	...	...	...	...		5 2	5 44	...	7 53
43½	Charlton Kings	„	.	9 20	10 44	.	.						2 0	V	.	.	.	.		5 9	5 51	.	8 0
44¾	Cheltenham (Sth.) & Leckh'pton	„	...	9 23	10 47	...	...						2 3	3 6	...	...	...	4 59		5 12	5 54	...	8 3
47¼	Cheltenham Spa (Malvern Road)	„	.	9 29		.	.						2 9	3 12	.	.	.	.			6 0	.	
47¾	**Chelt'ham Spa** (St. James')	arr	...	9 32	...	...	...						2 12	3 15	...	...	...	...		...	6 3	...	...
—	Chelt'ham Spa (Malv'n Rd.)	dep	.	9 52	.	.	.						2 42	3 26	.	.	.	.		.	6 16	.	.
—	Gloucester	arr	...	10 6	...	...	...						2 53	3 41	...	.	...	5 10		...	6 31	...	...

The Road Motor Services between Banbury and Chipping Norton, and Chipping Norton and Kingham, are liable to alteration. For particulars see local Omnibus announcements.

Week Days—contd. / Suns

		p.m.	p.m.	p.m.	p.m.	p.m.	Suns p.m.
			Saturdays only. ☞		Saturdays only. ☞	Thursdays and Saturdays only. ☞	
London (Paddington)	dep.	.	.	6C10	.	.	.
Oxford	„	4 40	...	6J30	...	*7 5*	...
Banbury	dep	5 35	.	7M40	.	*9 0*	.
King's Sutton	„	...	...	7 48	...	...	...
Adderbury	„	R	.	7 53	.	R	.
Milton Halt	„	...	...	P	...	...	...
Bloxham	„	5‡51	.	8 0	.	*‡16*	.
Hook Norton	„	6‡12	...	8 10	...	*9‡37*	...
Rollright Halt	„	6‡23	R	8 19	R	*9‡48*	R
Chipping Norton	arr.	6d35	...	8 25	...	*9d58*	..
	dep.		*8d0*	8 30	*9d5*		7d0
Sarsden Halt	„	...	...	P	...	☞	...
Kingham	arr.	.	*8 20*	8 40	*9 25*		7 20
Oxford	arr.	...	*9 15*	...			8Y12
London (Paddington)	„	.	*10 55*	.			9Y40
London (Paddington)	dep.	...		6Y5			...
Oxford	„	.		7 30			.
Kingham	dep.	...		8 55			...
Stow-on-the-Wold	„	.		9 4			.
Bourton-on-the-Water	„	...		9 9			...
Notgrove	„	.		9 20			.
Andoversford Junction	„	...		9 28			...
Charlton Kings	„	.		9 35			.
Cheltenham (South) & Leckhampton	„	...		9 38	...	...	...
Cheltenham Spa (Malvern Road)	„	.		.		.	.
Cheltenham Spa (St. James')	arr.	...		9 45		...	...
Chelt'ham Spa (Malvern Road)	dep.	.		10*10	.	.	.
Gloucester	arr.	...		10 26	...	...	...

Week Days.

		a.m.	a.m.	a.m.	a.m.	a.m.	a.m.	a.m.
						Mondays, Thursdays and Saturdays only.		
Gloucester	dep	5M40	...	...	...		..	9 56
Cheltenham Spa (Malv'n Rd.)	arr	5M*55	.	.	.		.	10 9
Chelt'ham Spa (St. James')	dep	6 32	...	...	...		...	10 35
Cheltenham Spa (Malvern Road)	„	.	.	.	.			10 38
Cheltenham (S'th) & Leckh'pton	„	6 38	...	...	...		10 35	10 45
Charlton Kings	„	6 43	.	.	.		10 40	10 50
Andoversford Junction	„	6 52	...	...	...		10 49	10 59
Notgrove	„	7 3	.	.	.			11 8
Bourton-on-the-Water	„	7 12	...	...	...		STOP	11 18
Stow-on-the-Wold	„	7 19	.	.	.			11 24
Kingham	arr.	7 27	...	...	...		...	11 32
Oxford	arr	8 30	.	.	.		.	12 38
London (Paddington)	„	9 50	...	...	...		...	2X10
London (Paddington)	dep	STOP	5 30	5 30	.		R	9 45
Oxford	„	a.m.	7 37	7 37	...		a.m.	11 15
Kingham	dep	7M49	8 25	9 0	.	☞	10 10	11 45
Sarsden Halt	„	7M 5	R	9 6	...			/
Chipping Norton	arr	8M 2	8d45	9 13	.	R	10d30	11 56
	dep	8M 3			10d2	*10 25*		
Rollright Halt	„	8M 9		.	.	*10‡37*	.	.
Hook Norton	„	8M17	...	...	...	*10‡48*	...	...
Bloxham	„	8M28	.	.	10‡29	*11‡9*	.	.
Milton Halt	„	8M32	...	...	...	...	...	...
Adderbury	„	8M36	.	.	R	.	.	.
King's Sutton	„	8M41	...	...	...	...	...	...
Banbury	arr	8M47	.	.	10 43	*11 25*	.	.
Oxford	arr	9J40	...	...	12 6	*12 21*	...	...
London (Paddington)	„	11J15	.	.	12 5	*2 10*	.	.

Week Days continued. / Suns.

																						Suns
		a.m.		a.m.	a.m.	p.m.	a.m.	p.m.	p.m.	p.m.	p.m.	p.m.	p.m.	p.m.	p.m.	p.m.	p.m.	p.m.	p.m.	p.m.	p.m.	p.m.
			Through Restaurant Car Train Swansea, Barry and Cardiff to Newcastle-on-Tyne.				Through Carriages Cheltenham Spa to London.	Thursdays and Saturdays only. ☞					Saturdays only. ☞					Saturdays only. ☞		Saturdays only. ☞	Thursdays and Saturdays only. ☞	
Gloucester	dep.	11 2		...	...	...	11 46	.	...	2 45	...	...	...	...	...	...	6 15	...	...	...	...	...
Cheltenham Spa (Malvern Road)	arr.	.		.	.	.	12 0	...	.	2 59	.	.	.	.	.	.	6 28	.	.	.	.	.
Cheltenham Spa (St. James')	dep.	...		...	...	...	12 10	...	...	3 16	...	...	...	...	...	...	7 5	...	...	...	...	...
Cheltenham Spa (Malvern Road)	„	.		.	.	.	12 12	...	.	3 20	.	.	.	.	.	.	7 8	.	.	.	.	.
Cheltenham (South) & Leckhampton	„	11 16		...	...	...	12 18	...	3 11	3 26	...	...	...	...	...	...	7 14	...	7 26	...	...	...
Charlton Kings	„	.		.	.	.	T	...	3 16	3 31	.	.	.	.	.	.	7 19	.	7 31	.	.	.
Andoversford Junction	„	...		...	...	...	12 30	...	3 24	3 39	...	...	...	...	...	...	7 27	...	7 40	...	...	...
Notgrove	„	.		.	.	.	T	...		3 48	.	.	.	.	.	.	7 36	.		.	.	.
Bourton-on-the-Water	„	Q		...	...	...	12 49	...	STOP	3 57	...	...	...	...	...	...	7 45	...	STOP	...	...	...
Stow-on-the-Wold	„	Q		.	.	.	12 54	...	.	4 3	.	.	.	.	.	.	7 50	.	.	.	.	.
Kingham	arr.	...		...	...	...	1 2	...	...	4 11	...	...	...	...	...	...	7 58	...	...	...	...	...
Oxford	arr.	.		.	.	.	1 39	☞	.	5 35	.	.	.	.	.	.	9 15	.	.	.	.	.
London (Paddington)	„	...		...	...	...	3Y0	...	p.m.	7 28	...	...	...	...	...	...	10 55	...	p.m.	...	...	...
London (Paddington)	dep.	.		.	9 45	.		*12U45*	12U45	STOP	1Y45	1Y45	☞	.	.	4Z45	.	*6Y5*	6Y5	☞		4 10
Oxford	„	...		...	11 32	...		*1 15*	*1b15*	...	3 50	3 50		...	...	6 8	...	*7 30*	7 30			5 50
Kingham	dep.	.		11 50	12M20	.		*2 25*	2 28	.	4 50	5M20	*6 3*	.	.	7 10	.	*8 20*	8M55	*9 35*		7 35
Sarsden Halt	„	...		R	12 26	...		*2 31*	R	...	R	5 26	*6 9*	...	R	R	...	R	9 1	R	☞	R
Chipping Norton	arr.	W		12d11	12 34	.		*2 38*	2d50	p.m.	5d11	5 33	*6 16*		.	7d31	.	*8d45*	9 8	*10d0*		8d0
	dep	...			12 36	12d41				3d23		5 36		6d26	6 37		...		9 11		*10d5*	
Rollright Halt	„	.		.	12 42	.		.	.	.	.	5 43	.	.	6‡49	.	.		9 18	.	*10‡15*	.
Hook Norton	„	...		...	12 49	...		...	...	...	...	5 50	...	...	7‡0	...	...		9 25	...	*10‡26*	...
Bloxham	„	.		.	12 59	1‡9		.	.	3‡51	.	6 1	.	6‡54	7‡21	.	.		9 35	.	*10‡47*	.
Milton Halt	„	...		...	1 3	...		...	...	...	...	6 6	...	...	...	...	...		9 41	...	...	...
Adderbury	„	.		.	1 7	R		.	.	R	.	6 12	.	R	.	.	.		9 47	.	R	.
King's Sutton	„	...		...	1 12	...		...	...	...	...	6 18	...	...	...	...	...		9 52	...	...	...
Banbury	arr.	12 40		.	1 18	1 21		.	.	4 4	.	6 25	.	7 7	7 37	.	.		10 0	.	*11 1*	.
Oxford	arr.	...	...	...	2 18	2 18		...	...	4 40	...	7 43	...	7 43	8 54	...	...		10 40	...	*11†50*	...
London (Paddington)	„	.	.	.	4 20	4 20		.	.	7 28	.	9 20	.	9 20	10 5	.	.		4¶10	.	*4†10*	.

A—Monday mornings excepted.
B—Calls at 4.25 p.m. to set down Passengers from Rugby and beyond on notice to the Guard at Banbury; also calls when required to pick up Passengers for Gloucester and beyond on notice at the station. Calls regularly on Thursdays to set down Passengers from Banbury.
C—Slip Carriage. **J**—Change at King's Sutton.
L—Calls at Bourton-on-the-Water at 4.31 p.m. to set down Passengers from Rugby and beyond on notice to the Guard at Banbury. Also calls on Thursdays to set down Passengers from Banbury.
M—Rail Motor Car, one class only.
N—Calls at Chipping Norton at 4.9 p.m. to set down Passengers from Rugby and beyond on notice being given to the Guard at Banbury. Also calls to pick up Passengers for Gloucester and beyond on notice being given at the station.
P—Calls to set down Passengers upon notice being given by the Passenger to the Guard at previous stopping station.
Q—Calls at Bourton-on-the-Water at 11.46 a.m. and Stow-on-the-Wold at 11.51 a.m. to pick up Passengers for Rugby and beyond on notice being given at the station.
R—Road Motor Service.
T—Calls to pick up Passengers for Reading and London on notice being given at the Station.
U—Luncheon Car, Paddington to Kingham.
V—Calls to set down Passengers from London on notice being given to the Guard at Kingham.
W—Calls at Chipping Norton at 12.5 p.m. to set down Passengers from Newport and beyond on notice being given to the Guard at Gloucester. Also calls to pick up Passengers for Rugby and beyond on notice being given at the station.
X—Restaurant Car between Paddington and Oxford, or vice versa.
Y—Restaurant Car between Paddington, Oxford and Kingham, or vice versa.
Z—Tea Car, Paddington to Oxford.
b—Thursdays and Saturdays only.
d—Chipping Norton Town Hall.
g—On Saturdays, depart Oxford 12.30 p.m.
*****—Cheltenham Spa (St. James'). †—a.m.
‡—Passes through Village.
¶—On Sunday mornings, arrive Paddington 2.40 a.m.

For Road Motor Service between Oxford, Andoversford and Cheltenham Spa see page 5B.
Road Motor Car Services are in operation between Banbury and Chipping Norton, Chipping Norton and Kingham, and Banbury and Swindon. (See Local Omnibus Announcements.)

Down Trains. BANBURY AND CHELTENHAM BRANCH. Week Days.

Double Line between Kings Sutton and Adderbury.
Single Line between Adderbury and Kingham East Box.
Double Line over Direct Loop between Kingham East and West Signal Boxes.
For particulars as to Staff Sections and System of Working see page 75.

Double Line between Kingham East Box and Kingham Station.
Double Line between Kingham Station and Kingham West Box.
Single Line between Kingham West Box and Andoversford Junction.
Double Line between Andoversford Junction and Cheltenham.

Time Allowances for Freight Trains see page 2.

Mile Post Mileage via King's Sutton M.	C.	Mile Post Mileage via Kingham M.	C.	STATIONS.	Ruling Gradient 1 in	Point-to-Point Allowances: Allow for Stop.	Allow for Start.	Vacuum.	Acc. "E"	Express.	Ordinary.	B Auto. arr.	B Auto. dep.	K Cattle, etc. MSO arr.	K Cattle, etc. MSO dep.	K Goods dep.	D Passenger. arr.	D Passenger. dep.	B Pass. dep.	K Goods. arr.	K Goods. dep.	G RR Light Engine
						Mins.	Mins.	Mins.	Mins.	Mins.	Mins.	a.m.	a.m.	a.m.	a.m.	a.m.	a.m.	a.m.	a.m.	a.m.	a.m.	p.m.
86	16	—	—	**BANBURY**									6 22									
84	2	—	—	**Astrop Siding Box**		1	1				5		—									
82	55	—	—	**King's Sutton**	L.	1	1				3		6 30									
—	—	—	—	**Sydenham Siding**									—									
84	08	—	—	**Adderbury**	180 R.	1	1			4	5		6 36									
85	42	—	—	**Milton Halt**	116 R.								6 42									
87	14	—	—	**Bloxham**	172 R.	1	1			7	8		6 48									
90	59	—	—	**Council Hill Siding**	100 R.	1	1				10		—									
91	37	—	—	**Hook Norton**	100 R.	1	1			11	2		6 58									
—	—	—	—	**Great Rollright Siding**	100 R.	1	1				9		—									
95	02	—	—	**Rollright Halt**	111 F.								7 7									
97	75	89	21	**CHIPPING NORTON**	80 F.	2	1			15	8	7 13	7L17	R	R				9 35			Z 12‖20
—	—	88	70	**Gas Works Siding**									—						—			—
—	—	86	47	**Sarsden Halt and Siding**	95 F.							7 22	7L24						9 40	Z		—
—	—	85	03	**Kingham (East) Box**	98 F.					9	10	C	S						CS			C12 29S
—	—	84	59	**KINGHAM**		1	1			1	1	7X29	—	—	7 45		—	8 38	9 45	—	10 15	—
—	—	85	28	**Kingham (West) Box**	80 F.	2 from Kingham E. / 1 from Kingham Stn.				2 from Kingham E. / 1 from Kingham W.		E 9.40 p.m. Souton Docks New Potatoes.		C7	X47 S		C	S	B 8.0 a.m. Ando'er Pass.	C	S	N12‖30
—	—	89	23	**Stow-on-the-Wold**	83 R.	1	1				12			C	R		8 46	8 48		10 29	10 55	K 10.15 a.m. Swind'n Goods
—	—	91	32	**Bourton-on-the-Water**	83 F.	1	1				5			7 59	8 10		8 52	8 54		11 2	12X 5	
—	—	96	38	**Notgrove**	60 R.	1	1				15			8 25	8 35		9 4	9 5	dep.	12X21C	T 1 28	
—	—	98	20	**Stop Board**	60 R.	1	1				4	a.m.	a.m.	8 40P	8 41		—	—	a.m.	1 33P	1 36	
—	—	101	10	**Andoversford Junction**	60 F.							R 2	R 17	C	S		C	S	10 42	C	S	p.m.
—	—	101	16	**ANDOVERSFORD**	L.	1	1				8	—	—	8X50	9 0		9 12	9 14	10 46	1 46	•2 27	Y1 40
—	—	101	28	**Stop Board**	76 F.		1			1	1	2 18	2P21	—	—		—	—	—	—	—	—
—	—	104	75	**Charlton Kings**	62 F.	1	1			8	8	—	—	C	R	9 14	—	9 21	10 53	2 38	•3 17	Z2 12
—	—	106	8	**Chel'h'm (S.) and Leck'h'n**	75 F.	1	1			3	3	—	—	—	—	CR	9 23	9 24	10 56	3 34	•4 10	CR
—	—	107	39	**Gloucester Loop Junction**	100 F.	1	1			3	3	—	—	—	—	—	—	—	—	4 15	P4 18	2P24
				Hatherley Junction	73 F.						2	—	—	9 18	P9*45	—	—	—	—	—	N	
A				**Lansdown Junction**	90 F.					1	1‡	2 38	2P41	—	—	9*23	9 28		10 59	4 20		2 27
				CHELTENHAM (Mal. Rd.)	216 R.	1				1	1			—	—	—	9 29	9 30	—	—	—	
See No. 7 Service Book.				**CHELTENHAM (St. James')**	168 R.							M	X	—	—	9 28	9 32	—		4 25		
				GLOUCESTER (Old Yard)	303 F.	1					13R			10 5	—							

L—Advertised Chip'g Norton 7.16 a.m., Sarsden Halt dep. 7.22 a.m.

Calls Leckhampton Sand Pit Sidings 3.21—3.31 p.m.

K'ham W. dep. 12.31, " Stn. arr. 12.33.

A—Distance Gloucester Loop Junction to Hatherley Junction, 39 chains. **R**—From Hatherley Junction. ‡—From Gloucester Loop Junction. **Y**—Arrive 1.24. **Z**—Arrive 1.51.

No. 15

Banbury and Cheltenham Branch—*continued.* Down Trains.

STAFF SECTIONS.

BETWEEN
Adderbury and Bloxham .. .. .. } Electric Train.
Bloxham and Hook Norton .. .. } Staff Section.

Hook Norton and Chipping Norton .. .. } Electric Train.
Chipping Norton and Kingham (East Box) } Staff Section.
Kingham (West) Box and Stow-on-Wold .. }

BETWEEN
Stow-on-Wold and Bourton-on-the-Water .. } Electric Train.
Bourton-on-the-Water and Notgrove .. .. } Staff Section.
Notgrove and Andoversford Junction Electric Train Tablet.

SARSDEN SIDING.—Sarsden Siding is not a Block Post. The Siding is locked by a key fixed in the end of the Electric Train Staff for the Section.

Running times for local passenger trains between Cheltenham and Kingham when load exceeds 100 Tons. See page 100.

Coupling of Goods, Ballast, and Mineral Trains, Bourton-on-the-Water to Notgrove.—Two Down Goods, Mineral, or Ballast Trains worked by ordinary engines may be coupled from Bourton-on-the-Water to Notgrove, in accordance with Rule 149a of the Book of Rules and Regulations.

Working of Trains via Hatherley Loop.—The drivers of all trains going from Gloucester in the direction of Kingham via Hatherley Loop must whistle **four times when passing Engine Shed Sidings Box at Gloucester.**

Drivers of all trains from the direction of Kingham going in the direction of Gloucester via the Hatherley Loop must give **one crow whistle when passing Andoversford Junction Box.**

Drivers of all Up Trains going on the Direct Line to Banbury must give one crow whistle when passing Notgrove Station.

Trains can be crossed at all stations on the Branch except at Stow-on-the-Wold.

WEEK DAYS. STATIONS.	B Auto. dep.	K Goods. arr.	K Goods. dep.	B Passenger. arr.	B Passenger. dep.	B Auto. dep.	K Goods. arr.	K Goods. dep.	B Pass. SO dep.	A 9.35 a.m. Newcastle to Swansea Passenger. arr.	A dep.	B Auto. dep.	E Gloucester Cattle. dep.	B Passenger. arr.	B Passenger. dep.	K 2.15 p.m. Sw'd'n Goods dep.	E New Potatoes. dep.	B 4.40 p.m. Souton Pass. dep.	B Auto. dep.	B Passenger. arr.	B Passenger. dep.	F 7.5 p.m. S. Dks. Goods dep.	D SUNDAYS Empty Auto. to Oxford dep.
	a.m.	a.m.	a.m.	p.m.	p.m.	p.m.	p.m.	p.m.	p.m.	p.m.	p.m.	p.m.	p.m.	p.m.	p.m.	p.m.	p.m.	p.m.	p.m.	p.m.	p.m.	p.m.	a.m.
BANBURY	10 30	—	10 40				—	2 5		3 30	3 37	4 5							7 40				
Astrop Siding	—	—	*10 49				—	—		—	—	—							—				
King's Sutton	10 38	10 52					2 15			3 42		4 13	RR						7 48				
Sydenham Siding	—	—	—				—	—		—	—	—							—				
Adderbury	10 44	11 0	11 20				2 21	2 51		C3	45S	4 19							7 53				
Milton Halt	1047½	—	—				—	—		—	—	4 23							R				
Bloxham	10X52	11 30	X12 25				3 1	3 16		C3	50S	4 29							8U0				
Council Hill Siding	—	C	R				—	—		—	—	—							—				
Hook Norton	11X 2	12 40	2X 0				3 31	—		C4	0S	4X38							8X10				
Great Rollright Siding	—	2 11	2 40							—	—	—							—				
Rollright Halt	11 11	—	—				B Passenger.			—	—	4 47							8 19				
CHIPPING NORTON	11 19	2 50	X5 35	—		12 50	arr.	dep.	3 12	VC4	9S	4 56							8 30				12†10
Gas Works Siding	—	—	—	—		—			—	—	—	—							—				—
Sarsden Halt & Siding	11 24	5 41	5 50	→		12 55	p.m.	p.m.	3 17	—	—	5 1							R				
Kingham (East) Box	CS	C	S			CS			CS	C4	17S	CS							CS				CS
KINGHAM	11 29	6 0	—	—	12 32	1 0	—	2 23	3 22	—	—	5X 6		—	5 10				8 40	—	8 55		12 20
Kingham (W'st) Box				CX	S		C	S		C4X	18S	B 2.40 p.m. And'ver pass.		C	S					C	S		
Stow-on-the-Wold		A—10.5 a.m. Southampton Passenger.		12 40	12 41		2 31	X2 32		Q4	25K			5 18	5 19					9 3	9 4		
Bourton-on-the-Water				12 45	12X50		2 36	2 37		QC4	31S		Y	5 23	5 25		RR			9 8	9 9		
Notgrove				—	1 1		C2	49SZ		C4	41S			—	X5 36					—	9 20		
Stop Board		p.m.	p.m.	—	—		—	—		—	—	p.m.		—	—					—	—		
Andoversford Junction		1 5		C	S		C	S		C	S	5 2		C	S	5 57	6 58	7 53		C	S	CR	
ANDOVERSFORD		—	—	1 8	X1 11		2 57	2 58		4 49		5 4	5 30	5 43	5 45	6 17	—	7 55		9 27	9 28		
Stop Board		—	—				—	—		—	—	—	—	—	—	—	7P2	—		—	—	11P46	
Charlton Kings		—	—	—	1 18		—	Z		—	—	5 11	—	—	5 52	—	RS	8 2		9 34	N9 36	—	
Chelt'm (S.) & Leck'h'n		—	—	—	1 21		3 6	3 7		4 57	4 59	5 14	—	5 54	5 55	—		8 5		9 38	N9 41	—	
Gloucester Loop Junct.		—	—	—	—		—	—		5 1		—	5P50	—	—	6 31	7P22	—		—	—	—	
Hatherley Junction		—	—	—	—		—	—		5 2		—		—	—	6P*56		—		—	—	—	
Lansdown Junction		1 14		1 25			3 11			—	—	5 17	5 53	5 59		—	7*25	8 8		9 45		12P 5	
CHELTENHAM (M.Rd.)				1 26	1 27		3 12	3 13		—	—		6 19	6 0	6 1	—				—	—		
CHELTENHAM (St. J's)				1 29	—		3 15	—		—	—		—	6 3	—	—				9 48	—		
GLOUCESTER										5 10	5 20		—			—	2.5 p.m. Sou'ton Docks						
GLOUCESTER (Old Yd.)													6 38			7 5							

To Oxford at 3.25 p.m.

Malvern Road arrive 5.56.

U—Bloxham treated as a Halt for this trip. Chipping Norton arr. 8.25 p.m.

Z—Guard to collect tickets, lock gates, and extinguish station lights.

K—Calls at Stow-on-the-Wold to pick up for Gloucester and beyond. **Z**—Calls if required to set down passengers from London. 3 minutes allowed for stops.

Q—Calls at Stow-on-Wold and Bourton-on-Water if required to set down passengers from Rugby and beyond. To call regularly at Stow-on-Wold and Bourton-on-Water on Thurs. to set down passengers from Banbury Market. 2 minutes allowed for stop. **R**—Calls at Milton and Sarsden Halts when required to set down passengers. **V**—Calls at Chipping Norton if required to set down passengers from Rugby and beyond on notice being given at Banbury, and to pick up passengers for Gloucester and beyond on notice being given at the station. **Y**—Runs alternate Fridays (Andoversford Stock Sale Days) to Gloucester Old Yard unless otherwise ordered.

No. 15

Up Trains. Banbury and Cheltenham Branch—*continued*. Week Days.

STATIONS.	Station No.	Ruling Gradient 1 in	Allow for Stop. (Mins.)	Allow for Start. (Mins.)	Vacuum. (Mins.)	Acc. "E." (Mins.)	Express. (Mins.)	Ordinary. (Mins.)	E✠ South'ton Goods dep.	E Goods. MSO RR arr.	E Goods. MSO RR dep.	B Passenger. arr.	B Passenger. dep.	B Auto. dep.	J Romsey Goods dep.
			Time Allowances for Freight Trains, see page 2. Point-to-Point Allowances.												
									a.m.	a.m.	a.m.	a.m.	a.m.	a.m.	a.m.
GLOUCESTER	—	178 R.	....	....	....	....	....	....	....	—	*5 45*	....	....	....	....
CHELTENHAM (St. James')	2612	—	..	1	..	..	..	..	..	—	—	—	**6 32**	..	..
CHELTENHAM (Mal. Rd.)	2609	168 R.	1	1	....	....	1	1	....	*6 7*	*6 18*	—	—	....	....
Lansdown Junction	2607	218 F.	..	..	..	..	1	1	4 10	*6 19*		6 34		..	7 41
Hatherley Junction	2606	—	....	....	....	....	....	....	—	—	—	—	—	....	—
Gloucester Loop Junction	6118	90 R.	..	..	..	..	1	2	—	*6 21*		—	—	..	—
Chel'h'm (S.) and Leck'h'n	6117	100 R.	1	1	....	....	4	4	—	—	—	6 38	6 39	....	—
Charlton Kings	6116	75 R.	1	1	..	..	4	4	—	—	—	—	6 44	..	—
ANDOVERSFORD	6115	62 R.	1	....	....	....	20	20	—	—	—	**6 51**	**6 53**	....	—
Andoversford Junction	6114	L.	..	..	..	..	..	..	4 37	C *6 36*	S	C	S	..	8 11
Notgrove	6112	60 R.	1	1	....	....	15	15		C	S	—	7 4	....	
Stop Board	—	L.	1	1	..	..	..	1	4.5 a.m. ex Cheltenham (High Street).	*6 48*	P*6 50*	—	—	..	7.35 a.m. ex Cheltenham (High Street).
Bourton-on-the-Water	6111	60 F.	2	1	....	....	10	10		*6 58*	P*7 0*	7 11	7 13	....	
Stow-on-the-Wold	6110	83 R.	1	1	..	..	..	5		C	S	7 17	7 20	..	
Kingham (West) Box ←■	6010	83 F.	....	....	....	....	14	9		C *7*	*11* S	CX	S	....	
KINGHAM	6006	80 R.	1	1	..	..	..	1		*7 13*	—	**7 27**	—	**7 49**	
Kingham (East) Box	6009	—	2 from Kingham W.			2 from Kingham W.								**C S**	
Sarsden Halt and Siding	6109	98 R.	..	..	..	1 from Station.				..	..	..	..	7 55	
Gas Works Siding	6108	—	....	....	....	....	....	....		....	....	....	....	—	
CHIPPING NORTON	6105	95 R.	1	2	..	..	9	12		..	..	..	..	**8 3**	
Rollright Halt	6103	80 R.	....	....	....	....	....	....		....	....	....	....	8 9	
Great Rollright Siding	6102	700 R.	1	1	..	..	..	10		..	..	..	..	—	
Hook Norton	6100	90 F.	2	1	....	....	14	10		....	....	....	....	8 17	
Council Hill Siding	6099	100 F.	1	1	..	..	5	2		..	..	..	..	—	..
Stop Board	—	100 F.	1	1	....	....	4	4		....	....	....	....	—	....
Bloxham	6098	100 F.	1	1	..	..	..	5	..	..	..	..	..	8X28	..
Milton Halt	6097	172 F.	....	....	....	....	....	....	....	....	....	....	....	8 32	....
Adderbury	6096	116 F.	1	1	..	..	6	8	..	..	..	..	..	8 36	..
Sydenham Siding	—	—	....	....	....	....	....	....	....	....	....	....	....	—	....
King's Sutton ←■	5006	180 F.	..	..	..	..	6	6	..	..	..	..	..	8 41	..
Astrop Siding	5007	—	1	1	....	....	....	3	....	....	....	....	....	—	....
BANBURY	5010	—	1	1	..	..	..	5	..	..	..	..	..	**8 47**	..

For special instructions see pages 74 and 75.

No. 15

Up Trains. Banbury and Cheltenham Branch—*continued*. Week Days.

STATIONS.	B Mixed. dep.	J Goods dep.	K Swindon Town Goods. arr.	K Swindon Town Goods. dep.	B South-ampton Pass. dep.	B Passenger. arr.	B Passenger. dep.
	a.m.	a.m.	a.m.	a.m.	a.m.	a.m.	a.m.
GLOUCESTER	....	....	—	**8 10**	....	....	....
CHELTENHAM (St. James')	..	..	—	—	..	—	**10 35**
CHELTENHAM (Mal. Rd.)	....	....	—	—	....	10 37	10 38
Lansdown Junction	..	8 10	—	—	10 30	10 39	
Hatherley Junction	....	—	—	**8*26**	—	—	—
Gloucester Loop Junction	..	—	8 28		—	—	—
Chel'h'm (S.) and Leck'h'n	....	—	—	—	10 35	—	10 44
Charlton Kings	..	**8 21**	**8 37**	**W8 57**	10 40	—	10 49
ANDOVERSFORD	....		**9 14**	**9 35**	**10 49**	**10 56**	**11 0**
Andoversford Junction	..				10 50	C	S
Notgrove	....	8.5 a.m. ex High Street.	....	....		—	11 9
Stop Board	..		..	..	..	—	—
Bourton-on-the-Water	....		....	....	....	11 16	11X19
Stow-on-the-Wold	..		..	..	..	11 23	11 25
Kingham (West) Box ←■	....		....	....	....	C	S
KINGHAM	**9 0**		..	..	..	**11 32**	—
Kingham (East) Box	**C S**		....	....	....	....	....
Sarsden Halt and Siding	9 6		..	..	..	..	..
Gas Works Siding	—		....	....	....	....	....
CHIPPING NORTON	**9 13**		..	..	..	..	..
Rollright Halt			....	....	....	....	....
Great Rollright Siding	..		..	..	..	..	..
Hook Norton	....		....	....	....	....	....
Council Hill Siding	..	..	..	..	..	..	..
Stop Board	....	....	....	....	....	....	....
Bloxham	..	..	..	..	..	..	..
Milton Halt	....	....	....	....	....	....	....
Adderbury	..	..	..	..	..	..	..
Sydenham Siding	....	....	....	....	....	....	....
King's Sutton ←■	..	..	..	..	..	..	..
Astrop Siding	....	....	....	....	....	....	....
BANBURY	..	..	..	..	..	..	..

STATIONS.	K Goods. arr.	K Goods. dep.	A 8.15 a.m. Swansea to Newcastle Passenger. arr.	A 8.15 a.m. Swansea to Newcastle Passenger. dep.	B Auto. dep.	F Cattle Empties. dep.
	a.m.	a.m.	a.m.	a.m.	p.m.	a.m.
GLOUCESTER	....	....	**10 58**	**11 2**	....	*11 55*
CHELTENHAM (St. James')	—	**10 46**	—	—	..	—
CHELTENHAM (Mal. Rd.)	—	—	—	—	....	—
Lansdown Junction	10 49		—	—	..	—
Hatherley Junction	—	—	11 11		....	*12 12*
Gloucester Loop Junction	—	—	11 12		..	*12*20*
Chel'h'm (S.) and Leck'h'n	**10 56**	**●11 25**	11 15	11 17	....	—
Charlton Kings	**11 31**	**11 55**	—	—	..	—
ANDOVERSFORD	**12 12**	**●1 8**	11 28		....	*12 45*
Andoversford Junction	**C**	**S**	**C**	**S**	..	
Notgrove	**1X23C**	**T1 38**	**C** 11	39 **S**	....	
Stop Board	**1 39**	**P1 42**	—	—	..	
Bourton-on-the-Water	**1 53**	**X 2 24**	**C** 11X	48 **SQ**	....	Runs alternate Fridays, Andoversford Cattle Sale Days. Gloucester Loop Junction arr.12.14.
Stow-on-the-Wold	**2X30**	**2 55**	**C** 11	53 **SQ**	..	
Kingham (West) Box ←■	3	5	**C** 11	59 **S**	....	
KINGHAM	**3 10**	—	—	—	**12 30**	
Kingham (East) Box			**C** 12	X0 **S**	**C S**	
Sarsden Halt and Siding			—	—	12 36	
Gas Works Siding	Shunts Dowdeswell Sidings.		—	—	—	
CHIPPING NORTON			**NC** 12	X8 **S**	**12 44**	
Rollright Halt			—	—	....	
Great Rollright Siding			—	—	..	
Hook Norton			**C** 12	18 **S**	....	
Council Hill Siding			—	—	..	
Stop Board			—	—	....	
Bloxham			**C** 12	X24 **S**	..	
Milton Halt			—	—	....	
Adderbury			**C** 12	29 **S**	..	
Sydenham Siding			—	—	....	....
King's Sutton ←■			12 32		..	..
Astrop Siding	....	....	—	—	....	....
BANBURY	..	..	**12‡37**	**12 44**	..	..

STATIONS.	B Passenger. arr.	B Passenger. dep.	B Auto. arr.	B Auto. dep.	A South-ampton Pass. dep.	B Passenger. SO arr.	B Passenger. SO dep.	B Andover Jct. Pass. dep.
	p.m.	p.m.	p.m.	p.m.	p.m.	p.m.	p.m.	p.m.
GLOUCESTER	....	....	....	....	....	....	....	....
CHELTENHAM (St. James')	—	**12 10**	..	..	..	..	..	..
CHELTENHAM (Mal. Rd.)	12 12	12 13	....	....	....	....	....	....
Lansdown Junction	12 14		..	..	1 36	..	..	3 6
Hatherley Junction	—	—	....	....	—	....	....	—
Gloucester Loop Junction	—	—	..	..	—	..	..	—
Chel'h'm (S.) and Leck'h'n	12 18	12 19	....	....	1 41	....	....	3 11
Charlton Kings	**V**	—	..	..	—	..	..	3 16
ANDOVERSFORD	12 30	12 31	....	....	—	....	....	**3 25**
Andoversford Junction	**C**	**S**	..	..	1 54	..	..	3 26
Notgrove	**VC** 12	X40 **S**	....	....		....	....	
Stop Board	—	—	..	..	..	..	..	..
Bourton-on-the-Water	12 48	X1250	....	....	....	....	....	....
Stow-on-the-Wold	12 54	12 55	..	..	..	..	..	..
Kingham (West) Box ←■	**C**	**S**	....	....	....	....	....	....
KINGHAM	**1X 2**	—	—	**1 20**	..	—	*2 25*	..
Kingham (East) Box			**C**	**S**	....	**C**	**S**	....
Sarsden Halt and Siding	..	..	—	1 26	..	—	*2 31*	..
Gas Works Siding	....	....	—	—	....	—	—	....
CHIPPING NORTON	..	..	**1 34**	**X1 36**	..	*2 38*	—	..
Rollright Halt	....	....	—	1 42	....			....
Great Rollright Siding	..	..	—	—	..	..	..	..
Hook Norton	....	....	—	1 49	....	....	....	....
Council Hill Siding	..	..	—	—	..	..	..	..
Stop Board	....	....	—	—	....	....	....	....
Bloxham	..	..	—	1 59	..	..	..	..
Milton Halt	....	....	—	2 3	....	....	....	....
Adderbury	..	..	—	2 7	..	..	..	..
Sydenham Siding	....	....	—	—	....	....	....	....
King's Sutton ←■	..	..	—	2 12	..	..	..	..
Astrop Siding	....	....	—	—	....	....	....	....
BANBURY	..	..	**2 18**	—	..	..	..	..

For Special Instructions, see pages 74 and 75.

N—Calls at Chipping Norton if required to set down passengers from Newport and beyond, on notice being given by the passenger at Gloucester, and to pick up for Rugby and beyond on notice being given at the station. **Q**—Calls at Bourton-on-Water and Stow-on-Wold if required to pick up for Rugby and beyond. 3 mins. allowed for stops. **R**—Does not run first Monday in month. **V**—Calls if required to pick up for Reading and London. 1 min. allowed for each stop. **W**—8.10 a.m. ex Gloucester assisted from Charlton Kings to Andoversford when required by Engine of 8.5 a.m. ex Cheltenham (High Street). ‡—Advertised arrival 12.50 p.m.

Up Trains. **Banbury and Cheltenham Branch**—*continued.* **Week Days.**

STATIONS.	B Passenger. arr.	B Passenger. dep.	B Auto. arr.	B Auto. dep.	K Goods. arr.	K Goods. dep.	K Goods and Cattle. SO arr.	K Goods and Cattle. SO dep.	K Banbury Junction Goods. arr.	K Banbury Junction Goods. dep.	B Passenger. arr.	B Passenger. dep.	B And-over Jct. Pass. dep.	B Auto. arr.	B Auto. dep.	B 10.55 p.m. Oxford Auto. SO arr.	B 10.55 p.m. Oxford Auto. SO dep.
	p.m.	p.m.	p.m.	p.m.	p.m.	p.m.	p.m.	p.m.	p.m.	p.m.	p.m.	p.m.	p.m.	p.m.	p.m.	p.m.	p.m.
GLOUCESTER								*4 40*									
CHELTENHAM (St. James')	—	**3 17**					—	—			—	**7 5**					
CHELTENHAM (Mal. Rd.)	3 19	3 21					**R**	**R**	—		7 7	7 8					
Lansdown Junction	3	22					—	—			7	9	7 21				
Hatherley Junction	—	—					*4*	*57*			—	—	—				
Gloucester Loop Junction	—	—					*4*	*59*			—	—	—				
Chel'h'm (S.) and Leck'h'n	—	3 27					—	—			—	7 14	7 26				
Charlton Kings	—	3 32					—	—			—	7 19	7 31				
ANDOVERSFORD	**3 39**	**3 42**					*5 17* **C**	**R** *5 25*			**7 26**	**7 30**	**7 41**				
Andoversford Junction	**C**	**S**					**C**	**S**			**C**	**S**	7 42				
Notgrove	—	3 51					**Cx**	**R**			7 38	7 40					
Stop Board	—	—					*5 51* **P**	*5 53*			—	—					
Bourton-on-the-Water	3 58	4 0					**C**	**R**			7 47	7 51					
Stow-on-the-Wold	4 4	4 6					**C**	**R**			7 55	7 58					
Kingham (West) Box ←■	**Cx**	**S**					**C** *6*	*18* **S**			**C**	**S**					
KINGHAM	**4 13**	—	—	**5 20**			*6 20*	—	—	**6 40**	**8 6**	—		—	**8 55**	*11 42*	*11 47*
Kingham (East) Box	━	━	**C**	**S**			━	━	—	—	━	━		**C**	**S**	**C**	**S**
Sarsden Halt and Siding			—	5 26					**6 46C**	**R6 56L**				—	9 1	—	*11 53*
Gas Works Siding			—	—					—	—				—	—	—	—
CHIPPING NORTON			**5 33**	**5 38**					**7 4**	**X 7 30**				**9 8**	**9 11**	*12 0*	—
Rollright Halt			—	5 46					—	—				—	9 18	━	━
Great Rollright Siding			—	—					—	—				—	—		
Hook Norton			—	5 53	—	**4 55**			**7 53**	**X 8 30**				—	9 25		
Council Hill Siding			—	—	**4 59**	**5 30**			—	—				—	—		
Stop Board			—	—	**5 36**	**P5 40**			**8 38P**	**8 41**				—	—		
Bloxham			—	6 5	**5 46**	**X 7 20**			**8 48P**	**9 10**				—	9 35		
Milton Halt			—	6 10	—	—			—	—				—	9 41		
Adderbury			—	6 17	**C** 7	23 **S**			**9 20**	**X9*35**				—	9 47		
Sydenham Siding			—	—	—	—			—	—				—	—		
King's Sutton ←■			—	6 23	7	45			9	42				—	9 52		
Astrop Siding			—	—	—	—			**9 47**	***10 50**				—	—		
BANBURY			**6 30**	—	**7 55**	—			**10 57**	**11 20**				**10 0**	—		

Goods and Cattle: Runs for six or more loads Live Stock or less if for more than two intermediate stations between Cheltenham and Kingham.

Andover Jct. Pass.: Andoversford arrive 7.39 p.m.

The Opening Ceremony

EXTRACT FROM BANBURY GUARDIAN

PUBLIC DINNER HELD IN THE TOWN HALL AT 3 PM. Dinner provided by Mr. Parker of the White Hart Hotel.

MENU

Port, Sherry and Champagne.

First Course

Quarters of Lamb – Shoulders of Lamb.
Dishes of roast beef.
Loins of veal – Hams
Dishes of chicken and tongue
Dishes of cutlets.
Dishes of sweetbreads
Dishes of hashed calves head
Pigeon pies
vol-au-vents
Dishes of curried rabbit – Green geese
Couples of ducks

Second Course

Cabinet puddings, plum puddings
Noyeau jellies, wine jellies
Creams, trifles
Dishes of pastry, tarts
Chicken salads, lobster salads

Dessert

Dishes of grapes, melons, pineapples, gooseberries,
Dishes of plums, French plums, almonds & raisins,
Dishes of biscuits, currants, raspberries, apples & cherries

This was certainly a 'scrumptious' meal to say the least!

The Mayor of Chipping Norton presided, supported by Sir S.M. Peto, Bart, John Parsons Esq., A.L. Rawlinson Esq., – Johnson Esq., the Mayor of Stratford-on-Avon, the Mayor of Banbury, Noel T. Smith Esq., John Fowler Esq., W. Lewis Esq., W. Rolls Esq., W.S. Hitchman Esq., H.G. Busby Esq., W.T. Adcock Esq., G.F. Tilsley Esq., Rev. James Morris, H. Wilkins Esq., Rev. A. Whishaw, Rev. Mr. Ellidge, – Spence Esq., Mr. E.R. Hartley, Mr. Holmes, and Mr. F. Sotham officiated as vice-presidents. Amongst the general company were Messrs Andrews, Arthur, Bent, T. Berry, Baker, Blackman, J. Biggerstaff, Dans, Edwards, Farnell, S. Guy, Gillam, Gibbs, Humphrey, Haywood (engineer), Hopgood, Keek, Loreland, R. Parsons, Pettapher, J.H. Stephens, Pearson, Page, W. Parsons, White, Shillingford, Sheppard, Huckvale, Keniber, Lockey, (surveyor), Pater, T.S. Hillier, R. Margetts, J.W. Lockwood, J. Hintt, T. Gulliver, C. Young, Whitehouse, Edwards, etc. After dinner the following ladies entered the room: Lady Peto, the Mayoress, Miss Peto, Mrs Kemp, Miss Broadbent, Misses Bliss (2), Mrs Whishaw, Mrs Tilsey, the Misses Kendall, Mrs & Misses Hitchman, Mrs H. Tilsey, Mrs Kingdon, Mrs Southam, Mrs Huckvale, Mrs Youngman, Mrs Hopgood, Mrs Keek, the Misses Guy, Mrs Morley, Miss Rolls, the Misses Rawlinson etc.

Order of proceedings

§ Chairman gave the toast "The Army and Navy" then the toast for "The County Members"!

§ Henry Wilkins, the ex-Mayor (Deputy Mayor), in an appropriate address, presented a very handsome silver salver and bread-basket to the Mayor, as a testimonial from his (the Mayor's) fellow-townsmen, neighbours, and friends, of their estimation of his private and public character, and particularly with respect to the invaluable services he had rendered in carrying the Chipping Norton Branch line to a successful completion.

§ The Mayor: Amongst other pleasantries he stated his love of his native place, that during the past 17 years in which he had resided in it, everything had tended to strengthen his love and attachment, not only to the town, but also to the people.

A proposal of a toast was made by him, "the health of the Directors of the OW&W Rly and success to the Chipping Norton branch". The toast was combined with one to John Parsons who had done much to promote the railway. These remarks were received with jubilant cheers.

One important point made was that: "As a railway it was not in itself a very important one so far as the general public was concerned, but it was in itself a sample, a picture, a beginning of a very important principle on which if branch railways were to be made, they must be constructed and carried out in order to make them more fairly remunerative to the shareholders and the promoters, than railways in years past have been".

Wlm Bliss the mayor then briefly and modestly told of the part he had played in the securing of the line and showing his gratitude to Sir Samuel Morton Peto and Mr. Fowler, who had risked their money and their time in the success of this undertaking. He went on to state the wishes of the OW&W Rly in wanting to accommodate the districts through which the line passed, but begged to state that they would not be in a condition for many years to come, to construct branch lines, and that the company were certainly indebted to the people of Chipping Norton for the spirit they had displayed, and the example they had given in the construction of this branch.

§ The Chairman next proposed, "The health of Sir Morton Peto, Bart", who had honoured them by his presence. "It was to him that they owed the commencement and carrying to a successful completion of their branch line." and that they would show their appreciation in the usual way.

§ Sir Morton Peto: Whose health had been given with all the honours, took the opportunity in returning thanks, of giving a short narrative of the circumstances attending his connection with the Chipping Norton line, which, as he observed, was a pattern which the promoters of our branch lines ought to follow. The days were past when landowners could obtain extortionate prices from railways for land; the days were gone when the promoters of lines were content to buy off the opposition of landholders by giving to them any amount or accommodation works they required, with also a most heavy price for land. He stated that he was an admirer of the late Sir Robert Peel in many respects, but that distinguished man never did so wrong as declining to attend to Lord Dalhousie's conservative principle, in the extension of the railway network of this country. Sir Samuel drew an illustration of how much money could have been saved.

Branch lines in this country were considered what was termed "suckers", and not "feeders" to main lines! Why? Because they had been projected to protect traffic or to annoy a neighbour, rather than with a view of developing the traffic of the districts through which they were constructed. He stated that because of the liberal-mindedness of the landowners, particularly Mr. Langston, the probability was that, instead of £6,000, the line would have cost from £12,000 to £15,000 per mile. "He thought that the principle on which this line had been constructed was one calculated to benefit the country through which branch lines passed; that it would give profit to the promoters and to the parent lines with which they were connected; and that such principle of construction would very largely stimulate the productive energies, and consequently increase the commerce of our common country" "London Illustrated News – Aug 18, 1855.

The Chairman proposed, "The health of John Fowler Esq., the eminent engineer of the OW&W rly". To him was owed the speedy completion of the undertaking.

John Fowler, Esq.,: He returned the thanks. In his opinion the inhabitants of the town were indebted to no one else but themselves. The conception and ultimate carrying out to its present state of completion of the Chipping Norton branch was undoubtedly due to Mr. Bliss whose perserverance and determination enabled them to complete the Chipping Norton railway. After more praise had been paid to William Bliss who had approached (John Fowler) about a prospective branch line, Mr. Fowler brought the important point of 'mixed gauges', a very controversial topic in 'railway politics' at the time. He stated that there had been some talk about the GWR compelling us (the OW&W rly) to lay down a broad gauge to Chipping Norton. They did not see much harm in it, because they did not mean to do it. Mentioning some minor failures, for instance of one or two useless expenses thrust on them, Mr. Fowler went on to state that he hoped shareholders might be spared useless expenditure in future. A parallel was then drawn between the Chipping Norton branch and the proposed branch line of the old plan to Stratford-on-Avon; the act for it being obtained in 1846, but owing to the stubborness of the landowners still had not been built. Praise for the principle in construction of the Chipping Norton line was great, especially with regard to the landowners on the line. (Mentioning apart Mr. Langston), whom he said, had taken great interest in the line and had spared no pains or labour, even when suffering under a serious affliction, to further it in everyway he could.

The Chairman: Explained the manner in which the scheme first originated. The praise was in reality due to Mr. Hitchman, who first inoculated him (the Major), with the necessity and importance of a railway to Chipping Norton. It was thought that £8,000–£10,000 should be raised for financing the railway, but ultimately on going to the railway officials the sum was more like £24,000, the agreement of which was that Chipping Norton should raise a third of the money, the company, the remaining two thirds.

The task of raising the money was set about and within three days various parties had subscribed one quarter of the amount, and in a fortnight the whole sum of £6,000, the prescribed one third, had been subscribed. The Chairman then said he went to the company to report his success, but that his spirits were somewhat dampened when told that a further £2,000 was required; however this was soon raised.

Sir Samuel Morton Peto: "The health of Mr. Rawlinson," proposed. Sir Samuel stated how highly he (Rawlinson) was respected by the inhabitants of Chipping Norton.

A. L. Rawlinson, Esq., in reply stated he was doing his duty as a professional man.

John Fowler Esq., then proceeded to toast, "The health of William Rolls Esq., and the Committee of the Chipping Norton branch railway, Messrs Bliss (chairman), Rolls (secretary), L. Guy, T. Keek, J. Loreland, T. Hopgood, J.H. Kingdon, and J. Ward,"

Mr. Rolls: Returned thanks on behalf of the committee of the Chipping Norton branch. He went on to state the "difficulties encountered" concerning the branch line – legal, pecuniary, open and concealed, but they had triumphed over all of them! Rolls stated that he was not prepared for the opposition which had long delayed the opening of the railway, much to th loss; and he could not refrain from saying that, from the high position in State of the gentleman who had been the cause of it, they could not have anticipated his throwing difficulties in the way of a spirited little town, struggling to maintain its position and to go forward with march of events

Why had they succeeded in overcoming difficulties? The unity of thos concerned, the determination and the assistance of the professional gentle men who had been connected with them were the main reasons outlined b Mr. Rolls.

At this juncture Sir S.M. Peto and the chief guests were obliged to leave the meeting, in order to proceed to London by the 6 o'clock train. On leaving meeting Sir S.M. Peto was loudly cheered. Mr. Hitchman occupied chair in the temporary absence of Mayor.

Mr. Hitchman: proposed the health of Mr. Langston, M.P., coupling it with the name of the Steward, Mr. Andrews, He went on to mention that he was sorry Mr. Langston could not be present because of his health.

H. Andrews Esq.: acknowledging the compliment, stated his pleasure in passing on to Mr. Langston their appreciation for his services. He hoped finally that, "the most sanguine expectations of the projectors of the line would be realised, and that little town would not only maintain its positic but would continue in the path of progressive improvements".

Mr. Hitchman: proposed the health of the Vice-presidents, coupling with the toast, the name of Mr. E. Hartley, Mr. Edw Hartley, returns the pleasantries.

The Mayor now resumed his post as chairman of the day, and proposed, "The health of the Mayor and Corporation of Banbury".

Richard Goffe, Esq.: responded in a humorous speech, stating that he was happy to find Chipping Norton such a go-ahead little town. He referred to the advantages derived from a railway in relation to Banbury in particular, and in conclusion said that he hoped the inhabitants of Chipping Norton would benefit from the new line.

Chairman: proposed the health of the Mayor and Corporation of Stratfor

–Warden Esq., responded: He stated that he had thought for some time that Stratford-on-Avon was left out of the world, in common with some other places without a branch line. Chipping Norton was the exception tc the rule, being blessed with persevering men and good luck. Stratford however was not without persevering men, who had been defeated on eve occasion by various parties squabbling about the mixed, narrow or broad gauge. He hoped that they might win out in time, especially since they had a population of 6,000.

R. Goffe Esq., proposed: "The health of the Mayor and Corporation of Chipping Norton.

The Mayor acknowledged the compliment on behalf of the Corporation present.

After implying their task in Chipping Norton had been an easy one, he stated that he thought there was some possibility of the line being extended to Banbury. Two or three gentlemen from Banbury had waited upon him with reference to a connexion of the branch with the Buckinghamshire line, but the Oxford, Worcester and Wolverhampton Co. could not sanction the scheme, (as he understood) unless it was continued to Cheltenham.

He hoped that the day was near when that junction would be effected

H.G. Busby Esq., proposed: "Prosperity to the town and trade of Chippir Norton"

The chairman, proposed: "The health of Mr. Lockey and officials connected with the branch line", to whom they were very much indebted

Mr Lockey, acknowledged the toast.

The Chairman then proposed: "The health of the landowners of the line," coupling with it the name of Mr. John Gibbs. He stated that the landowners had consented to give up their land in every instance, with only one exception, that of a nobleman who lived some miles away and who was therefore not so well acquainted with the importance of a branch line.

Mr. Gibbs acknowledged the compliment.

The Chairman then proceeded to toast, "The health of Mr. Wheeler, the station master", and expressed his satisfaction that although Mr. Whee had met with a serious accident, he was now present.

Mr. Wheeler replied to their pleasantries.

H. Wilkins Esq., proposed: "The Press", and Mr. Edw Hartley, "The Ladies", and terminated the interesting proceedings with an eloquent speech.

The Mayor entertained about 50 masons and carpenters, employed in the erection of his new factory on the common, at the Unicom.

The railway men and porters dined together at the Blue Boar; the band and constables at the Fox Inn. Mr. Hitchman's and Mr. Bickersta men were treated to a supper at the Blue Lion; and the ringers and others at the King's Arms.

Motive Power

Fig 228

Fig 229

All through this small book, I have endeavoured to show photographs which have included the engines and rolling stock used on the Banbury-Cheltenham railway over the years, but, as these were many and various, I have added several pictures and drawings here to substantiate the coverage and fill in the gaps. As mentioned before, in the historical section, the first engines known to have worked to Chipping Norton were Nos. 52 and 54, early 2-2-2 tanks made by Stephensons and although I do not have pictures, a drawing is shown on page 137. In Figure 228 the earliest photograph I can show, is of No. 177, one of the small 2-4-0 tanks made at Wolverhampton. The date of this Witney picture can be placed accurately as 1867, because after this No. 177 became No. 238! If this locomotive actually worked our branch or not cannot be known at this period in time, but the picture is included because she is typical of the type of engines which would have served.

No. 539 in Figure 229, however, is a certainty. She and many of her sisters worked both ends of the line, from Banbury, Cheltenham, Oxford and Worcester. In fact, many can be seen in the following pages. They belonged to the large class of 0-4-2 tanks known as the '517' series, built at Wolverhampton between the years 1868-1885 and repaired, altered and modified for another fifty years until superseded by the Collett '4800' class in 1932. The smaller picture at the top of this page is as near as I can get to the first 'Welsh Express' although not of the branch, or even of the train. This is surely what the original Swansea-Newcastle express must have looked like in 1906, with the Dean 4-4-0 at the head of the clerestory coaches. A marvellous sight. (Figure 230.)

Fig 230

Apart from the express, passengers on the Chipping Norton line were catered for mainly by the auto-car one class service, firstly in the shape of the steam rail cars and for nearly fifty years by the type of train seen in Figure 231. This is another '517' class engine, No. 847, with 70-foot Trailer No. 32. This photograph is typical of the 'between the years' service and is just how I remember the 'Chippy Flyer'.

Fig 231

Fig 232

From the Cheltenham end, occasionally would be seen the '3571' class of 0-4-2 tanks, as seen in Figure 232. These later developments of the '517's were built between 1895-7 and this particular engine, No. 3574, shedded at Worcester when I knew her, lasted until 1949!

Figure 233 shows one of the 2-4-0 'Barnum' class at the head of a horse box special. Many trains were known across the branch, both as race specials when Cheltenham was on the calendar, or as hunt specials, when the Heythrop were meeting at some station along the line.

Fig 233

Fig 234

The Banbury and Cheltenham branch was divided into two routes by the locomotive department. That between Banbury and Kingham was coloured *blue*, which meant a maximum axle loading of 17t.12c. on any one axle, this being decreed by the capabilities of the Hook Norton viaducts. The Kingham-Cheltenham section was a *red* route allowing a maximum of 20 tons per axle. All this, of course, determined the class of engine which could be used on the branch. A 'blue' engine used for the ore trains was the 26XX class, seen in Figure 234. These engines would work throughout the line in either direction.

As the section between Cheltenham and Andoversford Junction was used by the Midland and South Western Junction Railway, it is right to show these three examples of that railway's engine.

In Figure 235 is No. 8 in the original Midland and South Western Junction livery, and coupled to a 4-wheel 3rd class carriage of the 1890's. One of the North British Co.-built

Fig 235

4-4-0 engines is seen in Figure 236 after being absorbed in Great Western ownership in 1924 and rebuilt with Swindon boiler. This example was No. 7, later renumbered 1125 by the GWR.

Seen on Swindon shed in Figure 237, No. 1336 was MSW Junction's No. 12, built by Dubs in 1894 and was one of three numbered 10-12, later to become Nos. 1334, 1335 and 1336, all three lasted until 1952.

Other small engines in the 'blue' classification were the 'Duke' class which were often seen over the line with various types of train from excursions to Engineering Department Specials, Figure 238 (bottom) and the 'Bulldog' class, both curved framed, Figure 239, and the straight framed series, as seen in Figure 240 (both overleaf).

Fig 236

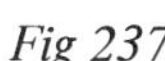

Fig 237

Fig 238

Fig 239

Fig 240

Fig 241

Many of the local goods trains were handled by the 0-6-0 Dean Goods, as seen in Figure 241. This was No. 2339, shedded at Worcester. In Figure 242, we have one of the largest freight engines which was used for the ironstone trains to South Wales. This actual engine is No. 3819, which was allocated to Banbury Shed.

Fig 242

Fig 243

Also seen across the branch after the 1930s were the Collett 0-6-0 locomotives of the '2250' class. No. 2299 is seen on shed in Figure 243 and in Figure 244 one of the 2-6-0 class which were also capable of handling anything on the line from the Newcastle express to the local pick-up goods. This one was No. 7318 seen taking water, on shed. Finally, moving to British Railways days, the 41XX series of large 2-6-2 tanks were used for many of the Kingham-Chipping Norton, Kingham-Cheltenham services; this picture shows No. 4128. (Figure 245 opposite.)

Fig 244

Fig 245

Fig 246

As mentioned before, the light branch type engines of the '517' class were finally replaced by Collett's '4800' class in 1932. These engines were renumbered in the 1940's into the '1400' series, and were used with the trailer cars, to carry on the tradition of the auto-car unit. No. 1421 is seen in Figure 246, being turned on a well type turntable. Figure 247 illustrates the largest passenger engine class to be worked across the Banbury-Cheltenham branch, the 'Manor' class. This particular example is No. 7819 *Hinton Manor.*

Five of these engines were stationed at Banbury depot, and the Newcastle-Swansea schedule was the first service on which these 'blue' engines were used. Lastly, the small 'Prairie' tanks, of the 45XX class, many of which were used on the Kingham-Cheltenham section of the line between the late 'thirties and closure. (Figure 248.)

Fig 247

Fig 248

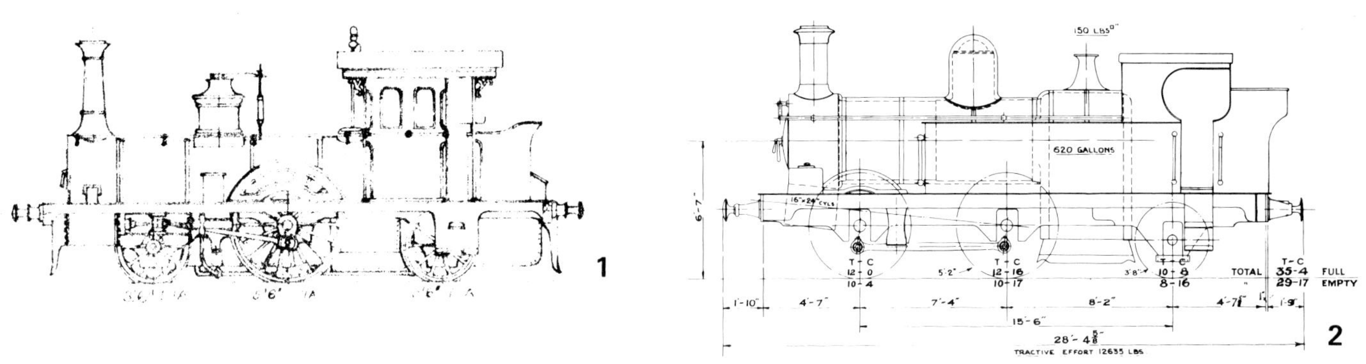

Outlines of Locomotives seen on the line

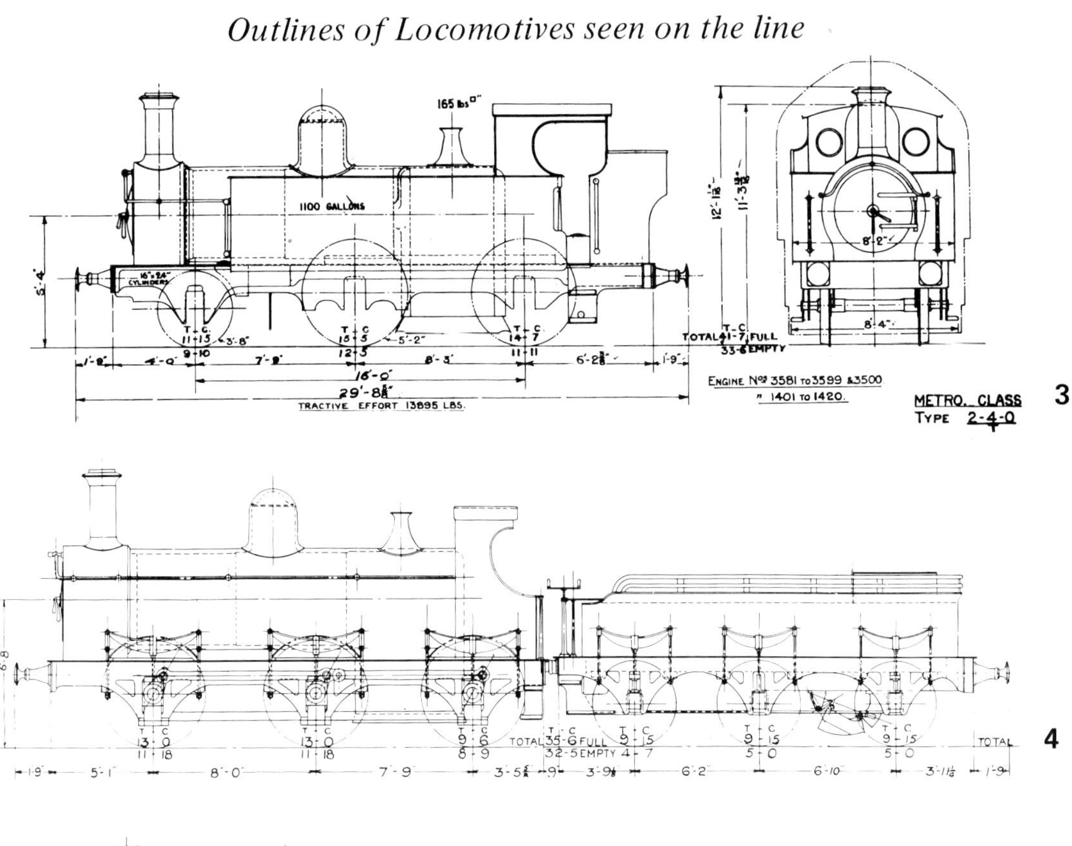

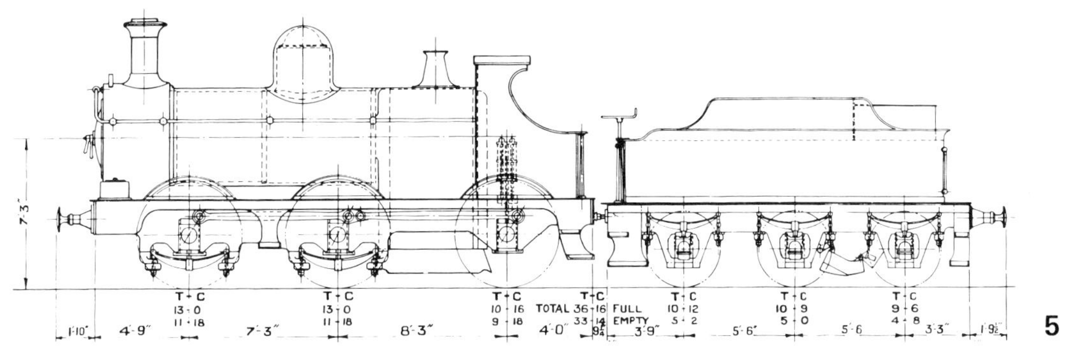

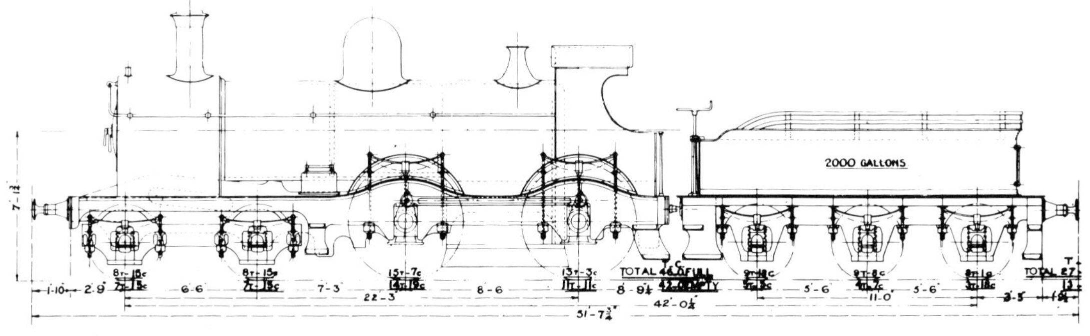

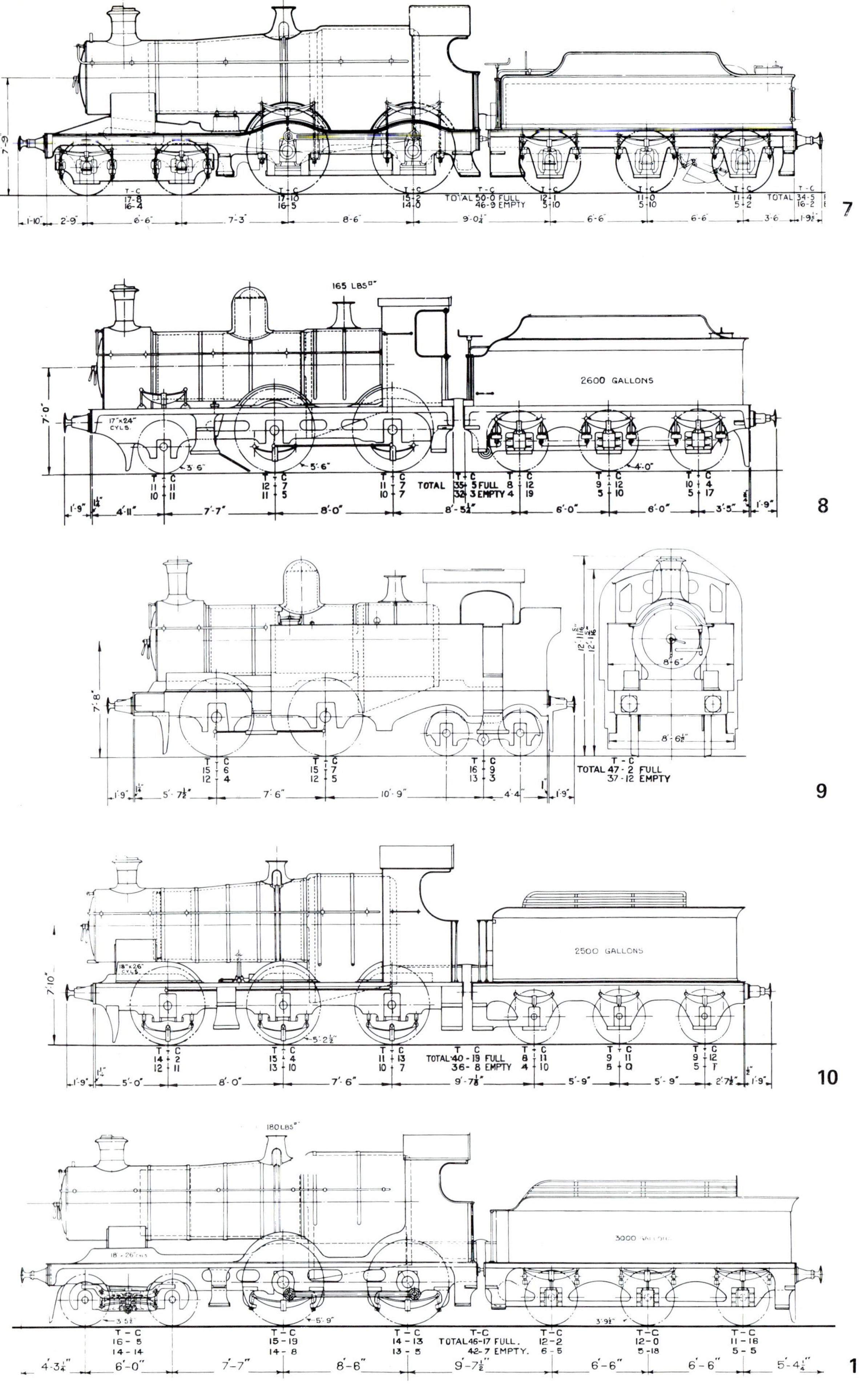

TOTAL 50-0 FULL
46-9 EMPTY
TOTAL 34-5
16-2
7
165 LBS□"
2600 GALLONS
17"x24" CYLS.
TOTAL 35-5 FULL
32-3 EMPTY
8
TOTAL 47-2 FULL
37-12 EMPTY
9
2500 GALLONS
18"x26" CYLS.
TOTAL 40-19 FULL
36-8 EMPTY
10
180 LBS□"
3000 GALLONS
TOTAL 46-17 FULL.
42-7 EMPTY.
11

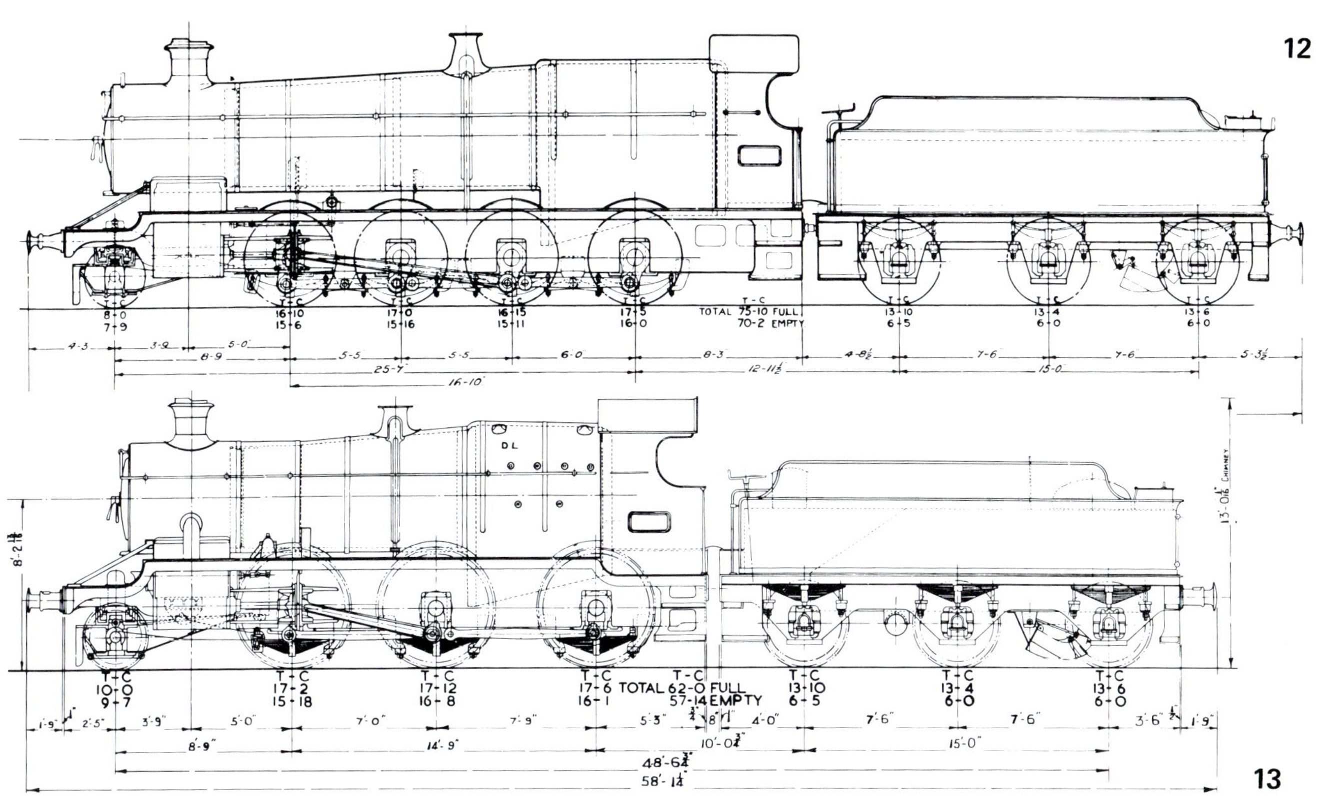

TOTAL 75-10 FULL
70-2 EMPTY
TOTAL 62-0 FULL
57-14 EMPTY
DL

12

13

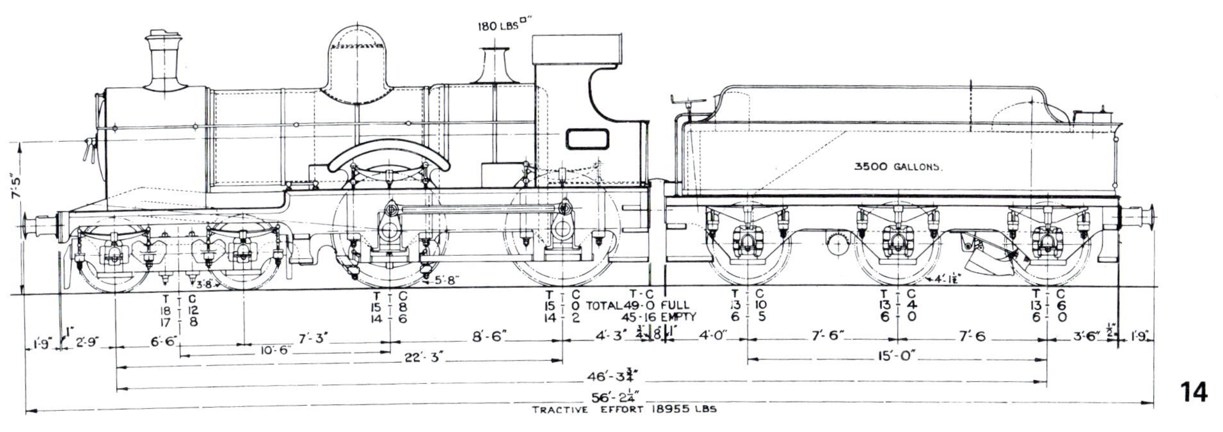

180 LBS
3500 GALLONS.
TOTAL 49-0 FULL
45-16 EMPTY
TRACTIVE EFFORT 18955 LBS

14

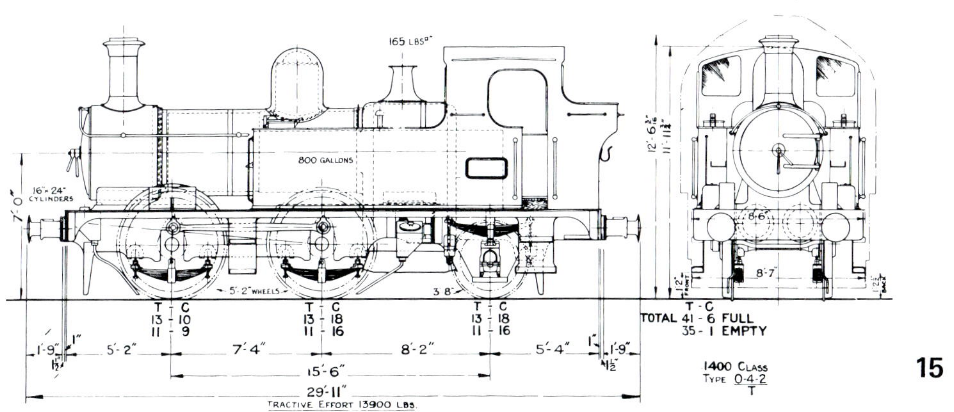

165 LBS
800 GALLONS
16"-24" CYLINDERS
5'-2" WHEELS
TOTAL 41-6 FULL
35-1 EMPTY
TRACTIVE EFFORT 13900 LBS
1400 CLASS
TYPE 0-4-2 T

15

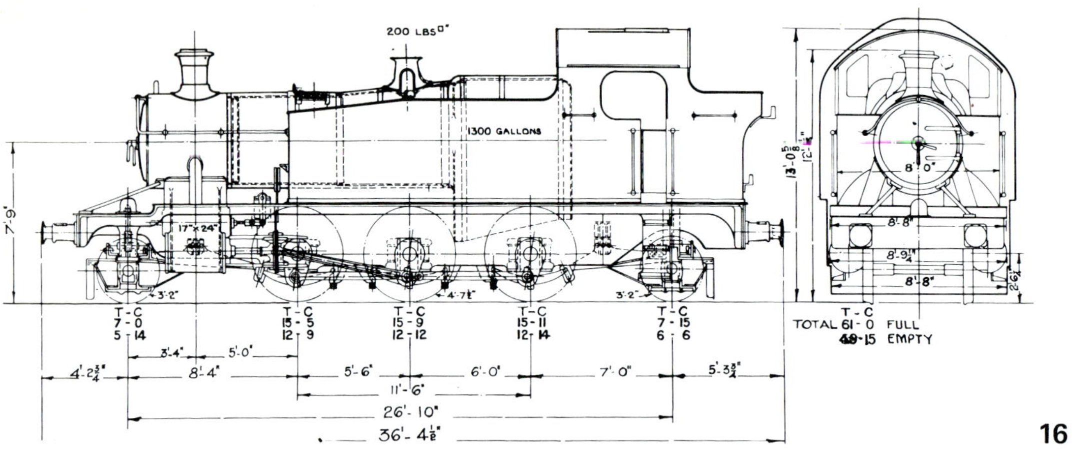

16

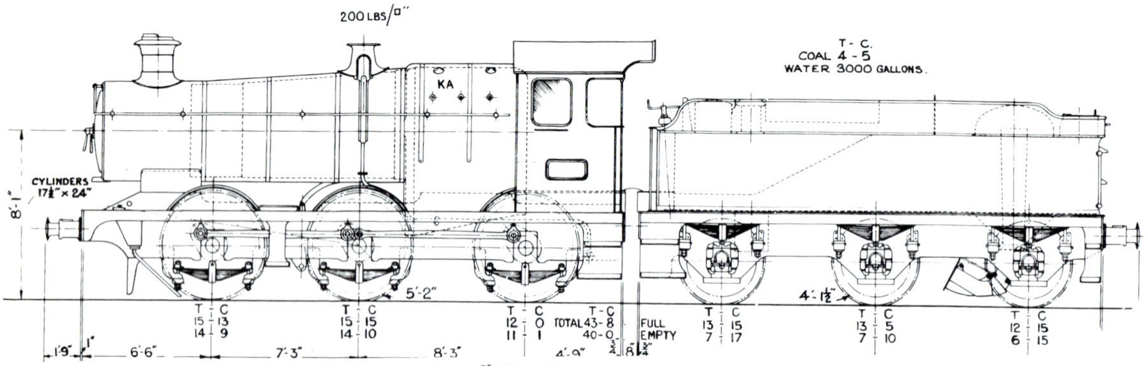

17

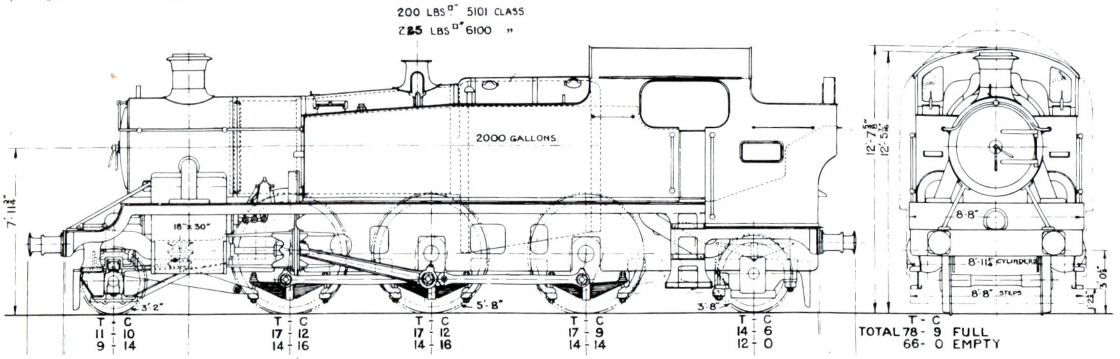

18

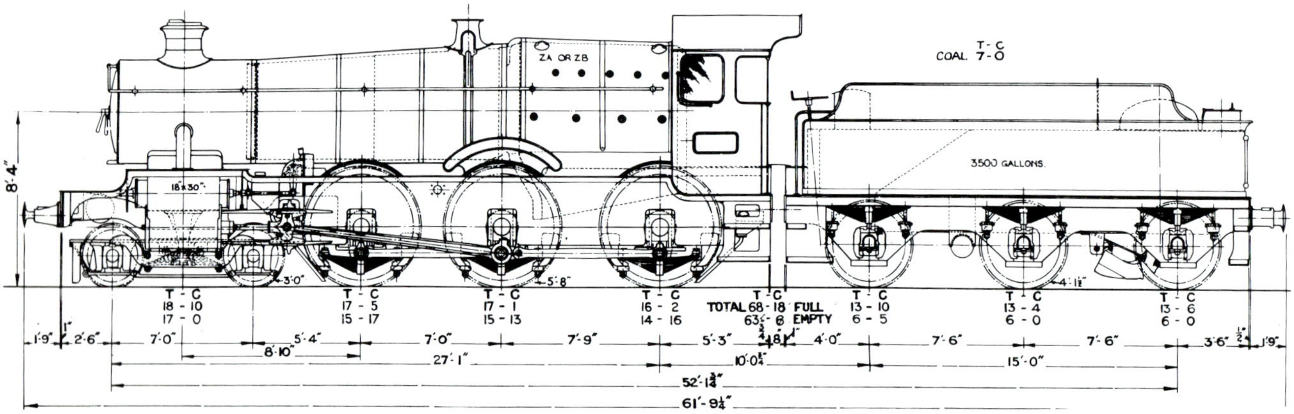

19

1. 2-2-2. Well tank. Built Stephensons.
2. 0-4-2. Side tank. '517' Class. Belpaire firebox.
3. 2-4-0. Tank Engine. 'Metro' Class.
4. 0-6-0. Armstrong Goods. '57' Class.
5. 0-6-0. Dean Goods. '2300' Class.
6. 4-4-0. 'Duke' Class. '3200' Class.
7. 4-4-0. 'Bulldog' Class. '3445' Class.
8. 2-4-0. Ex-MSW Jct. Rly. '1334'. Class series.
9. 0-4-4. Side tank Ex-MSW Jct. Same engine Swindonised.
10. 0-6-0. GW numbers 1003-13 Ex-MSW Jct.
11. 4-4-0. Engine MSW Jct. Rly. GW Nos. 1119-28.
12. 2-8-0. Heavy Freight. '28XX' Class.
13. 2-6-0. Mogul. '4300' Class.
14. 4-4-0. 'Dukedog'. '9000' Class.
15. 0-4-2T. 'Collett'. '4800' Class.
16. 2-6-2T. 'Small Prairie'. '4575' Class.
17. 0-6-0. Collett Goods. '2251' Class.
18. 2-6-2T. 'Large Prairie'. '5101' Class.
19. 4-6-0. 'Manor'. '7800' Class.